PROSPERITY
God's Way

Your Heavenly Father's Plan
to Bless You and
Make You a Blessing

DAVID CERULLO

PROSPERITY
God's Way

Your Heavenly Father's Plan to
Bless You and Make You a Blessing

by David Cerullo

Published by:

INSPIRATION MINISTRIES
PO Box 7750
Charlotte, NC 28241

+1 803-578-1899

inspiration.org

Printed in the United States of America.

DEDICATION

Dedicated to every Believer who yearns for a new beginning based on the promises of God's Word. May you walk in all the blessings your Heavenly Father has ordained for you...

...receiving His blessings so you can bless others
(Genesis 12:2)

...following His plan to gain wealth without sorrow
(Proverbs 10:22)

...living a life of overflowing abundance
(Psalm 23:5)

God's promises were written for *you*!

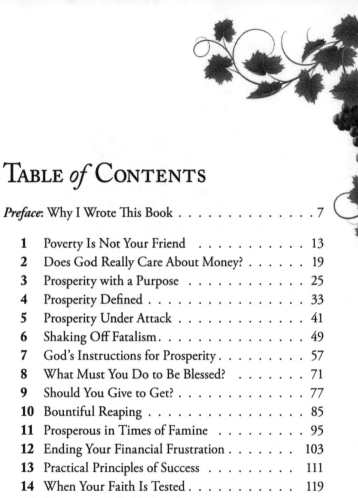

TABLE *of* CONTENTS

"Beloved, I pray that you may prosper in all things and be in health, just as your soul prospers."

– 3 John 1:2

WHY I WROTE THIS BOOK

Every day when we open the mail and email at Inspiration Ministries, there are hundreds of prayer requests from people in America and across the world who have serious financial needs.

My heart was moved with compassion when I read a letter from one woman who was so distressed about her finances that she wanted to die:

"David, my bills are piled high. I'm way behind on my house payment. I have a stack of bounced checks on the kitchen table, and I don't know where to turn."

And a man wrote:

"Please pray for me and my family. Our company recently downsized, and I was given a pink slip. I'm worried about my finances and how I will be able to provide for my wife and children."

Many people today are overwhelmed with debt and deeply troubled about their financial future. Perhaps you can relate.

What is God's plan to provide for us during such times? Sadly, some people just want to attack "the 1%"—those who are wealthiest—as the cause of their dismal financial situation.

But blaming or envying others is never the answer. No matter how bleak your current circumstances may look, God has a solution for you—a pathway to abundance and prosperity. And *no one* can stand in your way!

Why This Is Personal to Me

I know what it's like to experience financial problems. My wife Barbara and I have gone through difficult financial times of our own.

I know what it's like to be without a job. At one point, we literally had nothing—no money in the bank and none in our pockets. We didn't know how we were going to make our mortgage or car payments, nor did we even have money to buy groceries to feed our family.

One day we had to break open our son Ben's piggy bank just to have money for dinner. That was a stressful period, to be sure.

But through it all, we kept trusting God and applying His principles in our lives. Sometimes it was scary, but He met our every need. Now we can testify that the Lord has brought us from the Land of Not Enough to the Land of More Than Enough!

God Will Meet *Your* Needs Too

Just as the Lord has intervened to bless Barbara and me with financial breakthroughs, I'm confident He wants to come to your aid as well. As Paul wrote: *"This same God who takes care of me will supply all **your** needs from his glorious riches, which have been given to us in Christ Jesus"* (Philippians 4:19 NLT).

Paul had seen God's faithfulness in his own life, and he knew the Philippians would experience that same faithfulness. They had shown themselves faithful in supporting the word of God's Kingdom, and now they could be certain of God's covenant blessings.

Never forget: God is *Jehovah Jireh*, your faithful Provider (Genesis 22:14). When you put your faith in Him and obey His Word, He will never fail you.

But in order to be blessed with the overflowing abundance God wants to give you, you need to learn His principles of prosperity. Proverbs 10:22 promises, *"The blessing of the LORD makes one rich, and He adds no sorrow with it."* What a beautiful verse! While the world promotes all kinds of self-help routes to more wealth, the Bible promises you a regret-free pathway to prosperity, paved by *"the blessing of the LORD."*

Keys That Unlock His Kingdom

God's Kingdom is unshakeable (Hebrews 12:26-28), and His economic system is vastly different than the fickle economies of this world. Instead of relying on your job, your business, your bank account, or the stock market, the Lord wants you to look to HIM as your Source!

Regardless of the ups and downs of the world's economic system, there is never any lack in God's Kingdom. His Word promises: *"Those who seek the LORD shall not be in want of ANY good thing"* (Psalm 34:10) and *"No good thing does He withhold from those who walk uprightly"* (Psalm 84:11).

Yet the abundant blessings of God's Kingdom are not automatic. The Bible says there are *"keys of the kingdom of heaven"* (Matthew 16:19). Just as with any key, these Kingdom Keys are only effective when they are *used*.

I've written this book to share with you powerful Biblical keys for unlocking the prosperity and abundance of God's Kingdom. These principles are under fierce attack today, and you've probably heard some lies about the Scriptural principles God wants you to employ in order to receive His blessings. It's time to see what the Bible really says and set the record straight!

My prayer is that you'll take these principles to heart and practice them in your life. As you do, you'll see the hand of God move on your behalf to prosper you beyond your wildest dreams.

As the Apostle John prayed for Christians in the first century, so I pray for you:

> *"Beloved, I pray that you may prosper in all things and be in health, just as your soul prospers." – 3 John 1:2*

Praying God's best for you,

David

David Cerullo

"Christ has redeemed us from the curse of the law, having become a curse for us...that the blessing of Abraham might come..."

– Galatians 3:13-14

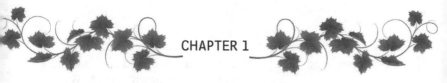

CHAPTER 1

POVERTY IS NOT YOUR FRIEND

While some preachers are accused of spending too much time instructing people on God's principles of abundance, most spend far too *little* time on the subject. Over the years, I've seen countless people's lives devastated by a *lack* of financial resources. Although we're not to center our lives on the pursuit of money, money clearly has an impact on every other aspect of our lives:

- Financial pressures are destructive to many marriages.

- Without adequate money, it's difficult to give kids the educational opportunities they need in order to achieve success.

- When money is tight, health and dental care may be deferred.

- With limited finances, it's difficult to do proper maintenance on our homes, cars, and other resources.

- When there's not even enough money to pay bills, it's very difficult to be a financial blessing to others or sow seeds to help fulfill the Great Commission.

- A lack of money can create a sense of disillusionment and bitterness in our relationship with the Lord.

So it's obvious that money has a powerful impact on many other areas of our lives. That must be why King Solomon concluded: *"Money is the answer to everything"* (Ecclesiastes 10:19 NASB).

Reversing the Curse

It's easier to understand what the Bible means by prosperity if you can picture how life was for Adam and Eve in the Garden of Eden: plentiful food, no financial lack, absence of any guilt or shame, and a harmonious relationship with the Lord and each other. Humankind only began to experience such hardships after their sin caused them to be under a curse (Genesis 3:17-19).

However, Jesus came to *reverse* this curse and grant us access to God's abundance again:

> *Christ has redeemed us from the curse of the law, having become a curse for us...that the blessing of Abraham might come upon the Gentiles in Christ Jesus...* (Galatians 3:13-14).

In contrast to this abundance offered to those who follow Him, Jesus says *"the thief"* comes to rob us of God's blessings (John 10:10). But there's good news! While poverty is a work of the enemy, Jesus came to *destroy* Satan's strongholds in our lives:

> *For this purpose the Son of God was manifested, that He might destroy the works of the devil* (1 John 3:8).

The Message paraphrases this:

> *The Son of God entered the scene to abolish the Devil's ways.*

Do you need the devil's works in your life to be destroyed? Then please understand: That's exactly what the Bible means by entering into God's prosperity—regaining a portion of what was lost when Adam and Eve were kicked out of the Garden.

We're Not to Be Paupers!

The next time you're tempted to criticize someone who's teaching God's people the Biblical keys to prosperity, remember how destructive poverty can be. As Solomon points out, *"Having no money **destroys** the poor"* (Proverbs 10:15 New Century Version).

Other translations use equally harsh words to describe the impact poverty has on people's lives: *"destruction"* (KJV, NKJV), *"ruin"* (NIV, NASB, ESV, RSV) and *"calamity"* (NLT). Is this what your Heavenly Father wants for you and His other children?

It's interesting that the Vulgate (Latin translation of the Bible) uses the word *pauperum* to refer to the poor. Of course, this is the root of our English word "pauper."

Think of it: God's beloved children living as "paupers"! In case you're a little hazy on what it means to be a pauper, here are definitions from several dictionaries:

1. One who is extremely poor, without any means of support

2. A destitute person who depends on aid from public welfare funds or charity

3. One living on or eligible for public charity

God forbid that *any* of this should be a description of you or loved ones. He hasn't called you to be a pauper!

Let's Get Angry

I don't know about you, but I get *angry* when I see Christians believing Satan's lies about prosperity and abundance. The consequences of believing these lies are always the same: destruction, ruin, calamity, and so much more. We're being robbed of our finances, marriages, health, and peace of mind, simply because we're missing out on God's prosperity.

Tragically, many of us seem to have made *peace* with poverty, either treating it as our friend or else trying to "peacefully coexist" with its dreadful impact. If you are one who has unwittingly done this, my friend, I urge you with all my heart:

**STOP! Poverty is your *enemy*, not your friend.
You need to go on the offensive and
banish poverty from your life!**

**Jesus died on the Cross to set you free from
every curse and *every* stronghold of the enemy.
You CAN enter into a new life of blessing
and abundance!**

Instead of feeling guilty about desiring a new level of abundance and prosperity, remember this: When God's people are blessed, His Kingdom is blessed and expanded—and this enables you to bless others as He has blessed you.

"Well done, good and faithful servant; you have been faithful over a few things, I will make you ruler over many things. Enter into the joy of your lord."

– Matthew 25:22-23

CHAPTER 2

DOES GOD REALLY CARE ABOUT MONEY?

Sometimes Christians are accused of being so Heavenly minded that they're of no earthly good. And I'll be honest: I've *met* some Christians who are like that! You probably have too.

Such "super-spiritual" Believers are likely to tell you God isn't concerned about money or any other earthly matters. His sole focus is on getting people saved so they can join Him in Heaven someday.

Yet, is that what the Bible advocates—a spirituality that focuses exclusively on our future life in Heaven, without addressing the "real world" issues of our life on earth?

No, the truth of the Bible pertains to BOTH time and eternity, as Paul points out: *"Godliness is of value in **every** way, as it holds promise for the present life and **also** for the life to come"* (1 Timothy 4:8 ESV).

Paul is saying the Lord has given us countless promises for our present lives, not just our Heavenly home. Not only has God *"blessed us with every spiritual blessing in the heavenly places in Christ"* (Ephesians 1:3), but He also wants to supply all of our needs while we're on earth (Philippians 4:19)!

He's Not Bashful About Money

I've noticed that many preachers seem reluctant to say much about money. Sure, they will have the obligatory "Stewardship Sunday" each year, but little is said about stewardship the rest of the year. And whenever the subject of money comes up, these timid preachers address the matter in an almost apologetic way.

In stark contrast, God has *never* been bashful in addressing the subject of money. In fact, it appears to be one of His favorite topics!

Since an estimated 2,300 verses in the Bible deal with how we should handle our money, it's pretty clear that this is a very important matter to God. Shouldn't it be important to us as well?

In both the Old and the New Testaments, God gives us instructions for handling our money and for being materially blessed in this present life. The book of Proverbs—written by King Solomon, probably the richest man who's ever lived—includes wisdom both for gaining material wealth and also for being a faithful steward of the resources God has already given us.

Sometimes an entire chapter, like Deuteronomy 28, describes the material blessings resulting from our obedience and the adverse consequences of our disobedience. And Paul spends the majority of 2 Corinthians 8 and 9 urging us to sow generous seeds into God's Kingdom and promising us blessings in return.

What Did Jesus Say?

Some commentators point to Jesus' warnings against greed (e.g., Luke 12:15) in an effort to prove He was opposed to people making a lot of money. However, the contexts of such warnings show that His point wasn't to discredit wealth but rather to encourage people to put their full reliance on the Lord.

Jesus taught that instead of being one who selfishly *"lays up treasure for himself,"* you should strive to be *"rich toward God"* (Luke 12:21). He promised that when you *"seek first the kingdom of God and His righteousness,"* you can be worry-free—for *"all these [material] things shall be added to you"* (Matthew 6:33).

Yes, Jesus taught that we should serve God rather than mammon (Matthew 6:19-24). But this was meant simply to free us from idolatry and encourage us to look to our Heavenly Father as our *source* of material blessings: *"For your heavenly Father knows that you need all these things"* (Matthew 6:22).

So Jesus wasn't being anti-wealth but simply pro-Kingdom. He wanted to set us free from the rat race of living for "things" instead of living for Him.

Jesus the Entrepreneur

If you need additional evidence that Jesus valued wealth and free enterprise, consider this: More than half of His parables had something to do with stewardship or money!

The Parable of the Talents, in particular, shows the master's displeasure when we bury our resources instead of investing them so that they increase in size (Matthew 25:14-30). Like us, the men described in the parable received differing degrees of material resources—but the master expected each of them to gain a return and increase his investment.

Instead of playing it safe, like the *"wicked and lazy servant"* did (Matthew 25:26), Jesus makes it clear the Father wants us to take risks and be entrepreneurial with the resources He's entrusted to us.

In the Contemporary English Version, this servant is called *"lazy and good-for-nothing"* (v. 26). *The Message* paraphrase helps us see the depth of the master's anger at this servant's timid lifestyle and failure to see the importance of investing the money:

> *The master was furious. "That's a terrible way to live!*
> *It's criminal to live cautiously like that! If you knew I*
> *was after the best, why did you do less than the least? The*
> *least you could have done would have been to **invest** the*
> *sum with the bankers, where at least I would have gotten*
> *a little **interest**"* (Matthew 25:26-27).

Echoing *The Message* translation here, I say to any Believers who are living this kind of fearful, overly cautious life: *"That's a terrible way to live!"* And not only is this a terrible way to live, but the ultimate consequences of living this way are quite perilous. In this parable, what does Jesus say to *do* with the unprofitable servant, who hid his talent and had no return or increase? He says to cast him into outer darkness, where there will be weeping and gnashing of teeth!

In numerous other passages—such as Matthew 25:14-30, Luke 19:11-27, Luke 16:1-15, Matthew 6:1-4, Luke 12:13-21—Jesus addresses a wide range of financial topics, such as giving, receiving, generosity, tithing, investing, giving alms to the poor, and long-term financial planning.

So the evidence is overwhelming: Our Lord never shied away from discussing money matters, and neither should we. Rather than discouraging wealth, He expects a return on His investment!

Instead of being timid in addressing financial issues, every true Bible teacher and minister of the Gospel has an *obligation* to teach God's people about what His Word has to say about financial giving and their tithes and offerings. You need to hear a clear message about the Lord's desire is for you to prosper and then be a good steward of your increase.

Faithful in Little Things

Not only does the Lord expect our financial assets to increase, but He also wants to give us *increased responsibility* as stewards of those assets. The master in the Parable of the Talents says to the two servants who increased his investment:

> *"Well done, good and faithful servant;* **you were faithful over a few things, I will make you ruler over many things.** *Enter into the joy of your lord." He also who had received two talents came and said, "Lord, you delivered to me two talents; look, I have gained two more talents besides them." His lord said to him, "Well done, good and faithful servant;* **you have been faithful over a few things, I will make you ruler over many things.** *Enter into the joy of your lord"* (Matthew 25:21-23).

When we prove ourselves faithful in a few things, God will entrust us with many things—a principle Jesus reaffirms in Luke 16:10-11 (NIV):

> *Whoever can be trusted with very* **little** *can also be trusted with* **much***, and whoever is dishonest with very little will also be dishonest with much. So if you have not been* **trustworthy in handling worldly wealth***, who will trust you with true riches?*

God uses our trustworthiness in *"handling worldly wealth"* as a huge barometer of whether He can trust us with greater responsibility in His Kingdom. This is just another indication of God's great interest in matters of money.

"You shall remember the Lord your God, for it is He who gives you power to get wealth, that He may establish His covenant which He swore to your fathers."

– Deuteronomy 8:18

CHAPTER 3

PROSPERITY WITH A PURPOSE

One of the most misquoted passages in the Bible is 1 Timothy 6:10. You've probably heard people say, "Money is the root of all evil," but that is not actually what this passage says.

Writing to his protégé, Timothy, the Apostle Paul warns: *"The love of money is a root of all kinds of evil."* Although the misquote may seem minor and harmless at first, the ramifications are profound.

The erroneous quote differs from the true quote in three primary ways:

- **"Love."** By leaving out the word "love," the misquote gives the false impression that money *itself* is evil. This is clearly not the case at all! If money is inherently evil, why would the master in the Parable of the Talents give it to his servants (Matthew 25:14-20)? And if wealth always leads its recipients to a downfall, why does the Bible tell us the Lord *"gives you power to get wealth, that He may establish His covenant which He swore to your fathers"* (Deuteronomy 8:18)?

- **"A root."** By saying **"THE** root" instead of *"A root,"* the incorrect translation gives the misleading impression that EVERY evil in the world is connected to money. No doubt, money has motivated greedy people to participate in many kinds of sinful behavior throughout human history: murder, fraud, theft, embezzlement, etc. But *other* "roots" of evil could be cited as well: such as lust, pride, envy, laziness, and anger. Jesus pointed to the *human heart* as a more fundamental source of evil than money or any other specific motivation: *"Out of the **heart** proceed evil thoughts, murders, adulteries, fornications, thefts, false witness, blasphemies"* (Matthew 15:19).

- **"All."** The correct translation of this verse is not **"all** evil" but *"all **kinds** of evil."* This is a significant difference. While the love of money can trigger evil behavior at times, it certainly doesn't cause ALL evil! Rather, Paul's point is simply that people's love for money and other material possessions can result in many different kinds of sinful behavior. Clearly so.

So the real issue is not whether or not people are rich, but rather whether people are setting their affection on their wealth or on God. Paul tells his protégé Timothy that wealthy people must be careful not to put their trust in their money:

> *Command those who are rich in this present age not to be haughty, nor to trust in uncertain riches but in the living God, who gives us richly all things to enjoy. Let them do good, that they be rich in good works, ready to give, willing to share, storing up for themselves a good foundation for the time to come, that they may lay hold of eternal life* (1 Timothy 6:17-19).

Notice that Paul didn't say rich Christians were in *sin* for having their wealth! He just wanted to make sure they were generous with what God had given them, quick to fund the work of the Gospel and reach out to those in need.

Paul didn't assume wealthy Christians *weren't* generous or *didn't* love the Lord. He simply wanted to remind them to keep their priorities straight.

In my experience, it seems that poor people are often even *more* in love with money than wealthy people. Why? Because from sunup to sundown, they find themselves obsessed with making ends meet. Living from paycheck to paycheck, having enough money becomes their main focus in life.

A Powerful Tool

Wealth is an extremely powerful tool, which can be used either for good or for evil. Godly people will use their wealth to spread the Gospel and bless others. Unrighteous people will use money as a tool for wickedness.

We also have many other "tools" that can be used either for good or evil, so money isn't really unique in this:

- **Printing presses** are used to print the Bible, newspapers, good or bad magazines and books, and pornography. A printing press isn't *inherently* good or bad, it's just a tool.

- **Electricity** is highly beneficial in providing us with light, heat, air conditioning, entertainment, and other things to enjoy. Even though some people get electrocuted each year because of using electricity improperly, there's no movement to ban electricity.

- **Cars** result in the deaths of more than 43,000 people each year in the United States alone, yet it's hard to find anyone who wants to go back to the days of the horse and buggy.

- **The Internet** is a powerful tool for spreading the Gospel, keeping in touch with friends, finding information, and spreading democratic ideals. But it's also a major tool for the spread of pornography and financial scams.

- **Television** has been a major tool of Satan, *"the prince of the power of the air"* (Ephesians 2:2), and he's used it to fill people's minds with hate, lust, immorality, and godlessness. However, Inspiration Ministries and other Christian TV networks are using the same tool to produce and broadcast programming to enrich people's lives and eternally impact them for Christ.

- **Nuclear energy** supplies electricity to millions of homes around the world, but it also can be used to create weapons of mass destruction.

You see, none of these things is inherently good or evil. Each one is merely a tool placed in our hands with a responsibility to use it wisely.

Just like these other tools, money can be used either for good or for evil. That's why Paul instructs Timothy that wealthy Believers should *"use their money to do good"* (1 Timothy 6:18 NLT).

A Personal Example

In 1990 Inspiration Ministries was born. It was quite a step of faith, but the Lord has honored it. Today hundreds of millions of people in the world have access to the Gospel of Jesus Christ through the media outreaches of Inspiration Ministries. In fact, every few minutes 24/7, we are hearing of someone, somewhere in the world, making Jesus Christ their Lord through this ministry!

Of course, none of this would have been possible if it hadn't been for the sacrificial giving of our partners. It takes LOTS of money to reach the world with the Gospel.

But whenever I think of the large cost of sending the Good News to the ends of the earth today, I remember an interesting story that took place after Jesus' Resurrection:

> *Some of the guard came into the city and reported to the chief priests all the things that had happened. When they had assembled with the elders and consulted together, they* **gave a large sum of money** *to the soldiers, saying, "Tell them, 'His disciples came at night and stole Him away while we slept.' And if this comes to the governor's ears, we will appease him and make you secure."*
>
> *So* **they took the money** *and did as they were instructed; and this saying is commonly reported among the Jews until this day* (Matthew 28:11-15).

You see, the opponents of the Gospel were willing to pay *"a large sum of money"* in order to spread lies discrediting Jesus' Resurrection. And the same is true today: Powerful financiers invest enormous sums of money to create movies, TV programs, and books to spread lust, obscenity, and lies that propagate evil or ridicule the cause of Christ. As God's people, shouldn't we, in return, be willing to spend large sums to spread the TRUTH?

We live in sobering times. Now more than ever, the Body of Christ needs to rise up and finance the End-Time Harvest of Souls. We need to sow sacrificial financial seeds to send the Light of the Gospel to the nations while it's still *"day"*—because the night is coming when no one can work (John 9:4).

This is just another example of how money can be a powerful tool either for good or for evil. People can invest *"a large sum of money"* either to spread the truth or to finance lies.

Loving the Lord

In the final analysis, the primary issue regarding money is

whether we love the Lord so much that He can *entrust us* with abundant financial resources. Just as you wouldn't entrust a car to your teen unless you were convinced they would drive responsibly, why should God entrust great financial resources to those who are untrustworthy stewards?

One of the reasons God gave great riches to Abraham is that He knew Abraham would be faithful to *"be a blessing"* to others (Genesis 12:2). He also demonstrated his understanding that *everything* he had was the gift of God:

- He tithed from everything he received (Genesis 14:18-20).

- He was willing even to put his dear son Isaac on the altar in loving obedience to God (Genesis 22).

So what about you? Are you more in love with the Lord than with the things He can give you? Do you seek the Giver more than the gifts?

God wants to bless you beyond your wildest dreams! As Peter experienced with the miracle catch of fish in John 21, the Lord wants to give you a miracle harvest far greater than you could ever expect. However, as He gives you this overflowing abundance, He will ask you the same question He asked Peter: *"Do you love Me?"* (vs. 15-17).

"If you then, being evil, know how to give good gifts to your children, how much more will your Father who is in heaven give good things to those who ask Him!"

– Matthew 7:11

CHAPTER 4

PROSPERITY DEFINED

Does God want to bless you with prosperity and abundance? Of course He does! What father would want his children to live in poverty and suffer lack?

Look at it this way: Earthly children are a reflection of their earthly father. In the same way, as Believers we are a reflection of our Heavenly Father. When people look at our lives, they're supposed to see the goodness and generosity of our Father.

Jesus was the perfect reflection of the Father, and He said, *"He who has seen Me has seen the Father"* (John 14:9). He also said *we* should be a reflection of that same nature: *"Know that I am in My Father, and you in Me, and I in you"* (John 14:20).

So what kind of living reflects better on the goodness of God? To have poor, naked, sick, dirty, homeless children, or to have children who are blessed, healthy, and prosperous?

The pages of Scripture are full of references to God as your loving Heavenly Father who wants to give you His best—everything you could ever need.

If you are willing to *"ask,"* *"seek,"* and *"knock,"* Jesus promises that your Father will gladly respond:

Ask, and it will be given to you; seek, and you will find; knock, and it will be opened to you. For everyone who asks receives, and he who seeks finds, and to him who knocks it will be opened.

Or what man is there among you who, if his son asks for bread, will give him a stone? Or if he asks for a fish, will he give him a serpent? If you then, being evil, know how to give good gifts to your children, how much more will your Father who is in heaven give good things to those who ask Him! (Matthew 7:7-11).

There are *hundreds* of similar Biblical promises about God's desire to bless and prosper His children when we walk in a covenant relationship with Him. Yet many Believers are not experiencing this kind of abundance.

Even worse, many actively *oppose* Biblical teachings on prosperity. When told about God's desire to bless them with abundance, they respond: "Oh, that's just 'name it and claim it.'" Or they say, "God chooses some people to abound and others to suffer lack—so no one can *demand* His blessings."

Misunderstanding the Message

Much of the confusion about prosperity and abundance stems from a failure to properly define them from a Biblical perspective. Critics often wrongly assume that advocates of the "prosperity message" are focused only on material blessings. "It's all about believing God for a big house or a Mercedes," they complain.

However, although God's prosperity certainly *includes* financial blessings, that is only a small part of what the abundant life is all about. In addition to providing His children with material abundance, the Lord wants to bless us with good health…strong relationships…peace of mind…victory over addictions…and most of all, an intimate relationship with Him.

God wants to bless us in every possible way: in our spirit, soul, and body…in our finances, marriages, children, health, and spiritual lives. The Apostle John describes this kind of all-inclusive prosperity like this:

> *Beloved, I pray that you may prosper in all things and be in health, just as your soul prospers* (3 John 1:2).

Do you see the amazing scope of the prosperity God desires for His children? His plan is not just to prosper us in some things, or just spiritual things: He wants us to *"prosper in ALL things"*!

Powerful Words

The Bible is full of powerful Hebrew and Greek words that testify of the incredible breadth and width of God's intended prosperity for His children. Here are some examples:

- **Blessing** (Hebrew *barak*) – "To bestow good upon." This word is used a remarkable 330 times in the Bible! A fundamental principle of Scripture is that God wants to BLESS His people and make them a BLESSING (Genesis 12:2). Opponents of the prosperity message fail to see that we first must *receive* God's blessings before we can pass them on to others.

- **Peace** (Hebrew *shalom*) – "To be made whole, healthy, happy, prosperous, and at peace." The Hebrew understanding of *shalom* is that it includes God's blessing in every area of our lives. It starts with peace with the Lord because of our covenant relationship with Him, but it then extends to our happiness, relationships, physical health, and financial provision.

- **Salvation** (Greek *sozo*) – "To be saved, delivered, healed, restored, or kept safe." Like the Hebrew word *shalom*, the

Greek word *sozo* speaks of God's desire to bring restoration to our entire being—spirit, soul, and body. When many Christians speak of "salvation," they focus only on their eternal reward in Heaven. Even though salvation (*sozo*) includes our eternal destiny, it ALSO refers to God's blessings in our present life: healing, deliverance, safety, and provision. Thus, when Mark 6:56 says, *"As many as touched Him were made well,"* the Greek word for *"made well"* is *sozo.* Those who touched Jesus in faith didn't only receive the right to go to Heaven when they died—they were made whole in every area of their lives.

- **Jesus** (Hebrew *Yeshua* or *Joshua*) – "The Lord (*Jehovah*) is salvation, deliverance, health, victory, liberty, and prosperity." The name of Jesus is powerful! Through the authority of His name we have access to all the covenant blessings of our Heavenly Father. In addition to receiving the forgiveness of our sins in Jesus' name (Matthew 1:21), His name brings us healing, deliverance, and prosperity (Acts 2:21, 3:16, 4:10, 4:12, 4:30, 10:43, 16:18). The Old Testament leader Joshua was called to lead God's people into the Promised Land—and he prefigured the work of Jesus, the Son of God, in bringing us into a covenant relationship with the Father.

- **Prosper** (Greek *euodoō*) – "To help on one's way, act wisely, and be successful and wealthy." Biblical prosperity stems from receiving God's wisdom and obeying His instructions on your journey. He promises that when you meditate on His Word and obey it, *"you will make your way prosperous, and then you will have good success"* (Joshua 1:8).

Based on these potent words describing the majestic scope of God's prosperity, it's very clear that the abundant life (John 10:10) includes much more than material wealth. If critics would recognize

the *totality* of God's desire to bless us, it would be much more difficult for them to reject the prosperity message as being unbalanced,
self-serving, or materialistic.

Understanding God's Nature

In the final analysis, the prosperity message is simply an exten-
sion of what the Bible says about the loving nature of our Heavenly
Father. One of His core traits is that He's a GIVER! (See John 3:16
and a multitude of other verses.)

The first thing God did after creating Adam and Eve was to
BLESS them! (Genesis 1:27-38). There were so many other ways
He could have begun His relationship with humankind, but He
chose to bless them, placing them in a beautiful garden, where they
had no lack.

Adam and Eve were placed in the Land of More Than Enough,
and that continues to be God's intention for His people. But instead of such a life, many Believers are living in the Land of Barely
Enough or Not Enough. Because of ignorance, unbelief, or disobedience, they forfeit God's intended blessings and live below their
inheritance in Christ.

If you are continually living with Barely Enough or Not Enough,
I have good news for you today: Your Heavenly Father loves you,
and He wants to bring you into a land of *overflowing abundance*. He
wants to overwhelmingly bless you so you can, in turn, be a great
blessing to others.

What does it look like to go from lack to abundance? In Matthew
14:14-21, Jesus' disciples had Not Enough to feed the thousands
of hungry people who had come to hear Jesus teach. But after they
brought the five loaves and two fish to Jesus from the little boy, a
miracle happened: Everyone had plenty to eat, and they ended up
with 12 full baskets of *leftovers*!

Jesus could have performed this miracle by just giving everyone enough to satisfy them. But He went *beyond* that and gave them an overflowing, "More Than Enough" miracle!

And notice that this turnaround didn't take long at all. Within mere moments, Jesus' disciples went from a place of lack to an experience of More Than Enough. And the same can happen for *you*...if you put your life and your resources into the hands of Jesus.

Believe and Receive!

If you don't *believe* in God's prosperity, it's unlikely you will *receive* His prosperity. Why? Because faith is an indispensable key to receiving the promises of God.

Jesus promises, *"It shall be done to you according to your faith"* (Matthew 9:29 NASB). What an incredible principle! If you believe God will prosper you...if you'll obey His commandments... if you'll be faithful to worship Him with your tithes and offerings... He will be faithful to bless you. But if you *don't* believe He will prosper you, He *won't*! Either way, He will honor your faith!

The story is told of a man during the Great Depression who lost his job and became homeless. Living on a street corner, he begged every day from those who passed by, hoping for enough change to buy a meal.

One day a wealthy man passed by and took pity on the homeless man. He stopped and wrote a large check, telling the man, "Here, this will help."

However, the homeless man looked at the check in disbelief, unable to believe that a total stranger would give him so much money. He put the check in his pocket and continued to beg, not comprehending how rich he had become.

My friend, like the homeless man in this story, in Christ you've become richer than you can even imagine. You don't have to keep begging, looking to the government or other people to meet your needs. God's Word says He's given you a huge check—with *your* name on it!

"Let the LORD be magnified, who has pleasure in the prosperity of His servant."

– Psalm 35:27

CHAPTER 5

PROSPERITY UNDER ATTACK

A fierce battle is raging today over the Bible's teachings about prosperity. Many well-meaning Christians have accepted the lie that God takes pleasure in giving them financial lack instead of abundance.

The consequences of this false belief system are tragic:

- God's children display poverty and lack instead of being a testimony of their Heavenly Father's faithful provision.

- Believers and their families undergo needless stress because of inadequate income.

- God's Kingdom receives inadequate funding to fully reach the world with the Gospel.

Those who criticize the Lord's offer of financial blessings typically attack two important principles found in Scripture:

- God's *desire* to bless His children with material things in this present life

- His prescribed *methods* for blessing His people

Like a hand in a glove, both of these must work *together* if God's prosperity is to be released in your life. It does little good to believe in the Lord's desire to bless you if you don't know and obey His instructions for *how* to receive those blessings.

Yet many Christians stumble over the very first step, because they're not really convinced of their Heavenly Father's intention to bless them. In contrast, look at what Scripture says about Abraham's walk of faith:

> *He did not waver at the promise of God through unbelief, but was strengthened in faith, giving glory to God, and being **fully convinced** that what He had promised He was also able to perform* (Romans 4:20-21).

Could this statement be made of you as well? Are you *"fully convinced"* the Lord is willing and able to bless you?

In order to receive God's abundance, James warns that we must…

> *…ask in faith, with no doubting, for he who doubts is like a wave of the sea driven and tossed by the wind. For let not that man suppose that he will receive anything from the Lord; he is a double-minded man, unstable in all his ways* (James 1:6-8).

The Lord wants you to get rid of any double-mindedness regarding His desire and ability to prosper you. You can bring Him your needs with full assurance of faith, without doubting.

God's Desire to Bless You

The Bible describes the devil as a thief (John 10:10) and a liar (John 8:44). Ever since the Garden of Eden, he has tried to slander God and convince people the Lord doesn't want to give them His best.

It all began when Satan planted a seed of doubt concerning the truthfulness of God's Word: *"Has God indeed said…?"* (Genesis 3:1). In the same way, the devil attempts to undermine your faith today by causing you to doubt God's promises to bless you.

A crucial ingredient in receiving God's abundance is accurately seeing Him as your loving Heavenly Father. That's why the enemy works so hard to discredit God's integrity and faithfulness.

Perhaps you're one of many who received a distorted view of your Heavenly Father because of negative experiences with your *earthly* father. If your earthly father lied to you…neglected you…abused you…abandoned you…or was stingy toward you, you may have a tendency to see God through that same distorted lens.

Yet Jesus taught that even *"evil"* earthly parents want their children to be blessed (Matthew 7:7-11). What parent would want their children to grow up poor, naked, uneducated, dirty, or hungry? Instead, we all want our children to grow up prosperous, well clothed, intelligent, well groomed, and well fed. How could God want anything less?

Psalm 35:27 declares: *"Let the LORD be magnified, who has **pleasure** in the **prosperity** of His servant."* That means you don't have to twist God's arm to bless you. He *delights* in seeing you and *all* His children prosper!

Yet some Christians seem convinced the Lord delights in their poverty…their suffering…and their distress. Nothing could be further from the truth.

If you subconsciously see God as a Scrooge or Taskmaster, you've got it all wrong. Ask the Lord to show you who He really is. Read His Word, enter His presence through worship and prayer, and spend time with Godly people who reflect the true character of your Heavenly Father.

Biblical Heroes Blessed by God

Throughout the Bible, we see people who were given great wealth as they honored and obeyed the Lord. Just to name a few, this list would include:

- Noah
- Abraham
- Isaac
- Jacob
- Joseph
- Boaz
- David
- Solomon
- Job

Should these men have renounced their material blessings and taken a vow of poverty in order to please the Lord? Certainly not. In fact, we're told that their prosperity came *from* the Lord, not just the result of their own efforts to get rich.

Were these men distracted from serving God because of their great prosperity? Although I'm sure that could happen to some people, we certainly don't see that in the lives of these Biblical heroes.

Let's take a closer look:

- **Noah** needed incredible material resources in order to obey God's commission to build the ark. From every indication, he was completely focused on his mission, taking little thought for his own pleasure or material comfort.

- **Abraham** *"was very rich in livestock, in silver, and in gold"* (Genesis 13:2), yet he realized he was *"blessed to be a blessing"* (Genesis 12:2). When he won great plunder after rescuing Lot, he gladly tithed to Melchizedek and refused to personally profit from what he had accomplished (Genesis 14:16-24). And later he was willing even to put his son Isaac on the altar in obedience to God and as a sacrifice of his worship (Genesis 22).

- **Isaac** demonstrated his trust in the Lord and his understanding of the principle of seedtime and harvest when he sowed seeds even in a time of great famine:

> *Isaac **sowed** in that land, and **reaped** in the same year a **hundredfold**; and **the LORD blessed him**. The man began to **prosper**, and **continued prospering** until he became **very prosperous**; for he had **possessions** of flocks and **possessions** of herds and a great number of servants. So the Philistines envied him* (Genesis 26:1, 12-14).

- **Jacob** discovered God's principles of abundance and *"became **exceedingly prosperous**, and had large flocks, female and male servants, and camels and donkeys"* (Genesis 30:43).

- **Joseph** continued to trust God despite the trials caused by his brothers' jealousy. As a result, he became one of the wealthiest and most powerful men in the world, controlling huge amounts of food and other resources:

  > *Pharaoh took off his signet ring from his hand and put it on Joseph's hand, and clothed him in garments of fine linen and put the gold necklace around his neck. He had him ride in his second chariot; and they proclaimed before him, "Bow the knee!" And he set him over all the land of Egypt* (Genesis 41:42-43 NASB).

- **Boaz** is described as *"a man of great wealth"* (Ruth 2:1), and he clearly was generous with his resources and kind to his servants.

- **David** was wealthy enough to lay up great resources for the Temple his son Solomon would later build (1 Chronicles 28:2-3, 11-19). Yet instead of allowing his wealth to distract him from his calling, David *"served the purpose of God in his own generation"* (Acts 13:36 NASB). The Lord gave him the ultimate endorsement, calling him *"a man after My own heart, who will do all My will"* (Acts 13:22).

- **Solomon** was the richest man who ever lived
  (2 Chronicles 1:11-12). Tragically, he strayed from God in
  his later years, but this was apparently not because of his
  wealth but because of the *"many foreign women"* he took as
  wives and concubines (1 Kings 11:1-10). Earlier, Solomon
  had set a powerful example of choosing to ask the Lord for
  "a wise and understanding heart" instead of wealth and honor
  (1 Kings 3:5-14).

- **The Nation of Israel** became extremely wealthy under
  King Solomon. He *"made silver and gold as plentiful in
  Jerusalem as stones"* (2 Chronicles 1:15).

- **Jehoshaphat** was one of Judah's best kings and *"had
  riches and honor in abundance"* (2 Chronicles 17:5).

- **Job** is described as having *"7,000 sheep, 3,000 camels, 500
  yoke of oxen, 500 female donkeys, and very many servants,"*
  and he was *"the greatest of all the men of the east"* (Job 1:3
  NASB). During a time of incredible testing, Job lost everything. Yet at the end of his ordeal, God restored him
  and gave him double of what he had in the beginning:

  > *The LORD **restored** the fortunes of Job when he prayed
  > for his friends, and the LORD **increased** all that Job
  > had **twofold**…The LORD blessed the latter days of Job
  > more than his beginning; and he had 14,000 sheep
  > and 6,000 camels and 1,000 yoke of oxen and 1,000
  > female donkeys* (Job 42:10-12).

You see, most of Israel's greatest heroes were rich rather than poor.
And we consistently see them *using* their wealth to be a blessing to
others.

Does God love the poor? Of course He does. But He loves them so much that He wants to bless them with greater abundance—NOT keep them poor!

So how does God reverse your fortunes if you've lived much of your life struggling financially, never seeming to have enough to make ends meet? As I describe in the next chapter, the turnaround will come when you learn to follow His instructions.

"May the favor of the Lord our God rest on us;
establish the work of our hands for us—
yes, establish the work of our hands."

– Psalm 90:17 NIV

CHAPTER 6

SHAKING OFF FATALISM

I once heard a preacher say, "The Bible says God causes some people to abound and others to be abased. If He wants me to struggle financially, there's little I can do about it—nor should I try."

This well-meaning pastor was basing his statement on a misquote of Paul's words in Philippians 4:10-13:

> *I rejoiced in the Lord greatly that now at last your care for me has flourished again; though you surely did care, but you lacked opportunity. Not that I speak in regard to need, for I have learned in whatever state I am, to be content: I know how to be abased, and I know how to abound. Everywhere and in all things I have learned both to be full and to be hungry, both to abound and to suffer need. I can do all things through Christ who strengthens me.*

Was Paul advocating the fatalistic view that some people are destined for prosperity, while others are destined for poverty? Not at all. In the context, he simply was pointing out that his joy and contentment weren't based on his temporary, external circumstances.

This is a lot different than saying God had destined him to forever remain in a certain economic station in life. If that were the case, he would have *continually* been abased and *never* would have abounded in prosperity.

Yet many Christians seem to share this preacher's fatalistic mind-set that our financial condition is predetermined by God and set in concrete. Such a view is akin to the Hindu caste system in India, where no one is allowed to improve his or her social strata, since it was predetermined by karma from their previous lives.

Do you see how destructive fatalism is? It negates personal responsibility for our decisions or actions. And since there's nothing we can do to change our financial destiny, fatalism always leads both to complacency and hopelessness.

From the Pit to the Palace

The Biblical worldview is radically different from fatalism. Rather than being inevitably stuck in our current position in life, God's Word offers HOPE that our lives can go from poverty to abundance if we trust the Lord and obey His teachings.

An entire book could be written on all the Biblical examples of people whose lives were transformed from failure to success…from poverty to prosperity…from defeat to victory…or from a pit to a palace. Here are just a few examples:

- **Joseph** spent time in the bottom of a well and years in a prison cell, before miraculously becoming the Prime Minister of Egypt (Genesis 37-50).

- **Moses** spent 40 years taking care of sheep in the wilderness before God raised him up to lead the Israelites out of slavery (Exodus 2-15).

- **David** was the youngest of Jesse's eight sons, and he seems to have gotten little respect from his brothers or even his father. Yet God raised him up from being a shepherd boy to being one of Israel's greatest kings (1 Samuel 16).

- **Mephibosheth** was a crippled beggar living in a desolate wasteland called Lo Debar before David brought him to the palace to live as one of his sons (2 Samuel 4:4; 2 Samuel 9).

- **Jabez** was called *"a pain"* at his birth, but he passionately sought God's blessing in prayer: *"Oh, that You would bless me indeed, and enlarge my territory, that Your hand would be with me, and that You would keep me from evil, that I may not cause pain!"* Instead of telling Jabez he was called to accept his lot in life and be abased, *"God granted him what he requested"* (1 Chronicles 4:9-10).

- **Peter** and several other disciples were fishermen, and at one point they told Jesus that they had *"worked hard all night and caught nothing"* (Luke 5:5). Yet when they obeyed Jesus' instruction, they suddenly went from great lack to great abundance.

Hopefully you can see from these examples that God doesn't preordain His people to remain in poverty. To the contrary, He's ready to give us amazing breakthroughs of abundance when we seek Him and obey His instructions.

God Expects an *Increase!*

The Parable of the Talents (Matthew 25:14-30) is such a helpful illustration of God's perspective on the resources He's entrusted to us. Did he *destine* one servant to have five talents, another to have two talents, and the final servant to just have one talent? NO! NO! NO!

Yes, the master initially gave the servants five, two, and one talent—but the whole point of the story is that he expected that initial investment to *increase*! That means the story could have turned out entirely different. For example, what if the first two servants were *content* with having five talents or two talents? What if they were the ones who buried what they had been given?

Think of how the story would have gone if the servant with one talent was the only one who invested what he had. Soon his assets would have grown *larger* than what the other two servants had!

So rather than the last servant being preordained to live in scarcity, this parable proves exactly the *opposite* point. Each of the servants had a *choice* to make about his stewardship—and he was rewarded or punished accordingly.

Blaming the Master

It's ironic that the unfaithful servant ends up blaming the master—instead of his own negligence—for his fate: *"Lord, I knew you to be a hard man, reaping where you have not sown, and gathering where you have not scattered seed. And I was afraid, and went and hid your talent in the ground. Look, there you have what is yours"* (vs. 24-25).

Sadly, this can be a typical response of those who continually live in poverty. Instead of accepting responsibility for their own choices and actions, they often look for someone else to blame for their plight. They may blame God, their boss, their spouse, the government, or the economy—but they'll find *someone* to hold responsible for keeping them poor.

But the master in this parable refuses to listen to any of this rationalizing. Instead, he holds the final servant squarely to blame for the consequences of his actions, calling him a *"wicked and lazy servant"* (v. 26). In contrast with the other two servants, who were *"good and faithful"* (vs. 21, 23), this servant was clearly *"unprofitable"* (v. 30).

You might think the master would feel sorry for the unproductive servant, but that wasn't his reaction at all. He was ANGRY! He had the right to expect a return on his investment, and the final servant grievously let him down.

It's interesting that in Jesus' concluding words about this parable, He speaks about abundance: *"To everyone who has, more will be given, and he will have abundance"* (v. 29). The message is clear: *Anyone* can end up with abundance, but he must invest what God has given him, so it will grow.

Misunderstanding Contentment

The Parable of the Talents also dispels a commonly accepted myth about contentment.

I'm always puzzled when I meet Christians who tell me they don't think it's right to ask God to prosper them. "David," they say with a certain smugness, "the Bible says to be content with what we have, and that's what I'm doing."

Sometimes they go on to quote a variety of Scriptures on the subject, like these:

> *I have learned to be content in whatever circumstances I am* (Philippians 4:11 NASB).

> *Let your conduct be without covetousness; be content with such things as you have. For He Himself has said, "I will never leave you nor forsake you"* (Hebrews 13:5).

> *Godliness with contentment is great gain. For we brought nothing into this world, and it is certain we can carry nothing out. And having food and clothing, with these we shall be content*
> (1 Timothy 6:6-8).

But based on the Parable of the Talents, I believe many of us have misunderstood what contentment really means. Does it mean we just lie down and resign ourselves to our current lot in life? That's a *horrifying* thought! If everyone had adopted this warped view of contentment, consider what the consequences would have been:

- **Moses** would have told the Israelites to mind their business and remain as slaves in Egypt.

- **Christopher Columbus** would have been satisfied with the existing trade routes—and the New World wouldn't have been discovered for many years to come.

- **George Washington, Thomas Jefferson, Benjamin Franklin, and America's other Founding Fathers** would have repented of any notion they should overthrow the British and establish a new nation.

- **Abraham Lincoln** would have remained in poverty in Illinois instead of becoming an attorney and then running for national office. And instead of signing the Emancipation Proclamation, he would have advised the slaves to be content with their preordained station in life.

- **George Washington Carver** would have been content to remain a slave or an impoverished tenant farmer. Instead, he continually furthered his education and became a famed scientist, botanist, educator, and inventor whose ideas revolutionized agriculture in the southern United States. He created about 100 different products from peanuts, including cosmetics, dyes, paints, plastics, gasoline, and nitroglycerin.

- **Orville and Wilbur Wright** would have been content to run their bicycle shop instead of pursuing their dream of inventing a functional airplane.

This list could go on and on and on. World-changing leaders

clearly have NOT been content just to maintain the status quo.

So, What Is *True* Contentment?

One of the central messages of the Parable of the Talents is that God doesn't want us to be content just to maintain whatever He has given us. The *"unprofitable"* servant *tried* that approach, remember?

Instead, God expects a return on His investment in our lives. And that only happens when we invest our resources into *"good ground"* where they will reap a harvest and increase.

So it's fine to be grateful for the resources God has already given us, but we must realize they're meant to be just a *seed*—able to grow and multiply when they're planted.

And it's wonderful to maintain a contented *attitude*, for the Bible teaches us to *"do all things without complaining and disputing"* (Philippians 2:14). As Paul points out, the Israelites who complained *"were destroyed by the destroyer"* (1 Corinthians 10:10).

However, contentment must never be an excuse for laziness or a lack of vision for our lives. Instead of displaying an apathetic, passive, or unmotivated lifestyle, we must *press toward the goal for the prize of the upward call of God in Christ Jesus"* (Philippians 3:14). Otherwise, we will have nothing to show the Master when He returns.

So are you ready to shake off your excuses, get unstuck, and find a new level of prosperity and blessing from God? Your turnaround starts with a decision to believe God's promises instead of Satan's lies or your present circumstances.

"*Give, and it will be given to you: good measure, pressed down, shaken together, and running over will be put into your bosom.*"

– Luke 6:38

CHAPTER 7

God's Instructions for Prosperity

When you were a kid, did you ever receive a great toy for Christmas, only to find that it didn't seem to work? Perhaps you hurriedly yanked off the wrapping paper, ripped open the package, and pushed the start button—but with absolutely no response.

"What's wrong with it?" you wondered. "Is my new toy broken already?"

In all likelihood, your nifty new Christmas present failed to work for one basic reason: *You failed to read and follow the instructions!*

In the same way, although it's exciting to hear about God's promises for a life of abundance, many Believers find themselves disappointed when they don't immediately receive their eagerly anticipated prosperity. Typically, they blame God for not being true to His Word, but the real problem is much simpler: *They didn't take time to learn and follow His instructions!*

Friend, never forget:

Although God's love for you is unconditional, His *promises* nearly always are tied to *conditions* you must follow in order to receive the desired blessing.

Is there a promise in God's Word you claimed, without receiving the desired result? Then I encourage you to go back and look at the context of the Scripture passage again. What condition or instruction did the Lord include with His promise?

Throughout the Bible, you'll find God saying, *"I'll* do this…if *you'll* do that."* Ask Him to show you any ways you've missed the mark in doing *your* part to receive His provision.

God's Prescribed Methods to Bless You

Even after becoming convinced of God's desire to bless them, many people still fail to actually *receive* the anticipated blessings. Often we expect God's provision to automatically and immediately fall from the sky, just because we've prayed and believed.

While it's certainly possible for the Lord to supernaturally provide for us by dropping manna, quail, or some other provision out of the sky, this is seldom how He chooses to work. Rather, He works through established principles of abundance, which He has set forth in His Word.

For example, one of God's primary methods of blessing His people is through the principle of seedtime and harvest, which is a very simple concept:

> *Whatever a man sows, that he will also reap* (Galatians 6:7).

> *He who sows sparingly will also reap sparingly, and he who sows bountifully will also reap bountifully* (2 Corinthians 9:6).

The principle of seedtime and harvest is not only found throughout Scripture, but it's also an established law of nature. What farmer would expect to harvest a crop if he hasn't first planted any seeds?

Yet many of us try to claim God's amazing covenant blessings, even when we're not faithfully sowing seeds into His Kingdom! Once our seeds are sown, He is able to bless and multiply them.

But it's impossible for a harvest to start until something is *sown*!

Seeds That Bring a Harvest

The Bible is clear: If you're going to discover the full measure of God's covenant blessings, you must understand, accept, and practice the principle of seedtime and harvest. The size and scope of your harvest will always be in proportion to your faith and the seeds you sow.

Although the principle of seedtime and harvest is one of the clearest precepts in the Bible—first mentioned in the creation account (Genesis 1:11)—it's under vicious attacks by critics. "It's selfish and materialistic," they argue, "to think you should GIVE in order to GET!"

Yet Jesus Himself teaches this very thing:

> *Give, and it will be given to you: good measure, pressed down, shaken together, and running over will be put into your bosom. For with the same measure that you use, it will be measured back to you* (Luke 6:38).

And instead of being just a random principle that God honors from time to time, the Bible says seedtime and harvest is an enduring law that will continue as long as the earth exists:

> *While the earth remains,*
> *Seedtime and harvest,*
> *Cold and heat,*
> *Winter and summer,*
> *And day and night*
> ***Shall not cease*** (Genesis 8:22).

What farmer indiscriminately goes out into the field and simply tosses his seed here and there and goes away with no expectation to come back at a later time and reap a harvest? Not one!

The wise farmer sows with *intent*, not indiscriminately. He sows with eager *expectation*, not nonchalantly.

So what are you waiting for? If you want to receive a future harvest, there's no better time than today to start planting seeds! The critics will pass away, but the law of seedtime and harvest will remain.

Various Kinds of Offerings

Perhaps you've never given much thought to your offerings to the Lord. But you *should*, because Scripture frequently ties God's promises of financial prosperity to our faithfulness to bring Him the prescribed offerings.

In fact, almost all the activity of the Tabernacle in the wilderness and the Temple in Jerusalem centered around the sacrifices of God's people and the giving of tithes and offerings. Throughout the Bible, giving was always an important part of the worship prescribed for God's people.

However, this principle has been lost in many churches today. Often when churches come to their time to give tithes and offerings, it's a hurry-up kind of thing, as if they can't wait to get it over with. Yet it certainly wasn't done that way in Bible times.

The principle of seedtime and harvest includes various kinds of offerings we can give to the Lord, and the Bible is full of references to these offerings. But for right now, I want to focus on just two of these: our tithes and our special offerings during God's three "Appointed Times."

Tithes. A tithe literally means "a tenth." Throughout Scripture, God instructs us to give Him 10% of all our increase, saying the tithe is "holy" to Him:

> *All the tithe of the land, whether of the seed of the land or of*

the fruit of the tree, is the LORD's. It is holy to the LORD
(Leviticus 27:30).

Critics love to claim that tithing was just a requirement under the Old Covenant Law and therefore isn't relevant for today. What a terrible twisting and complete misunderstanding of Scripture.

The principle of tithing predated the Law by nearly 500 years! Abraham paid tithes to Melchizedek (Genesis 14:3), and the practice was continued by Isaac, Jacob, and the other forefathers over 400 years *before* Moses ever received the Law on Mount Sinai.

It's also misguided to say Jesus did away with tithing or other principles of giving and worship from the Old Testament Scriptures. He *commended* the scribes and Pharisees for tithing, though He criticized them for neglecting *"the weightier matters of the law"* (Matthew 23:23).

And Jesus specifically refuted the claim that His mission was to abolish the Law:

> *Do not think that I came to destroy the Law or the Prophets. I did not come to destroy but to fulfill. For assuredly, I say to you, till heaven and earth pass away, one jot or one tittle will by no means pass from the law till all is fulfilled* (Matthew 5:17-18).

God says the tithe is His, and we rob Him if we fail to tithe. How can He bless our lives if we don't freely give Him what is already His?

Malachi 3:8-12 clearly ties our prosperity to our obedience in giving the Lord tithes and offerings:

> *Will a man rob God? Yet you have robbed Me! But you say, "In what way have we robbed You?" In tithes and offerings. You are cursed with a curse, for you have robbed Me, even this whole nation.*
>
> *Bring all the tithes into the storehouse, that there may be*

*food in My house, and try Me now in this, says the LORD of
hosts, if I will not open for you the windows of heaven and
pour out for you such blessing that there will not be room
enough to receive it. And I will rebuke the devourer for your
sakes, so that he will not destroy the fruit of your ground,
nor shall the vine fail to bear fruit for you in the field, says
the LORD of hosts. And all nations will call you blessed.*

My friend, do you see how God's amazing promises are tied to
your faithfulness to bring Him tithes and offerings that are right-
fully His, not yours? He's not promising to give you Barely Enough,
but rather More Than Enough—blessings that overflow into the
lives of others. In addition, He offers to *"rebuke the devourer"* from
stealing His blessings from your life.

Sadly, a study by pollster George Barna revealed that only **8%**
of born again Christians give tithes from their income—and 16%
give no donations at all! Is it any wonder so many Christians have
financial problems?

Special Offerings at God's Appointed Times

Some of the Lord's most incredible spiritual blessings are
offered to us through the Biblical feasts ordained in Exodus 23 and
Leviticus 23. These passages describe three Holy Convocations…
"Appointed Times"…seasons when God wants to meet with His
people and bless our lives in miraculous ways.

Referring to these three feasts—Passover, Pentecost, and Taber-
nacles—Deuteronomy 16:16 says, *"None shall appear before the LORD
empty-handed."* Yes, God put conditions on His promises, and He
decreed that these three appointed feasts are to be celebrated *per-
petually* throughout all generation…FOREVER (Leviticus 23:41).

These aren't *Israel's* feasts or the *Church's* feasts—they're the
Lord's feasts!

His instructions about the feasts aren't tied to an old or a new covenant. He simply tells us emphatically: *"Three times you shall keep a feast to Me in the year"* (Exodus 23:14). This was a direct and insistent command!

Jesus celebrated the feasts. The disciples celebrated the feasts. The Apostle Paul celebrated the feasts. The early Church celebrated the feasts. So it's misguided to think these feasts are irrelevant to Believers today.

Let me be clear: Celebrating these Appointed Times has *NOTHING* to do with your salvation, but it has a *LOT* to do with releasing God's covenant blessings in your life!

Each one of us needs God's supernatural…

Guidance	**Provision**
Healing	**Victory**
Protection	**Restoration**

These are just a few of the covenant promises God made to His children in Exodus 23…*if* they would obey Him in all He asked.

Think about it. Israel never had a big army compared to the armies of their enemies. But they weren't depending on the size of their army—they were depending on the size of their GOD and His PROMISES to deliver them!

God was faithful to His Word. He supernaturally provided for them in the wilderness. He gave them food and water, and even kept their shoes from wearing out. Israel lived under a canopy of God's covenant promises to give them supernatural abundance and blessing—the same provision we need in our lives today!

The Israelites KNEW that if they obeyed the Lord…kept His commandments…and came before Him with their tithes and special offerings, they could depend on God to keep His promises to bless them.

Of course, Scripture is clear that the Lord is the rightful Owner of *everything* in Heaven and on earth (Psalm 24:1, 1 Chronicles 29:11). But there's something very special about the offerings God commanded them to bring during these feasts. He said they were to be in *addition* to their tithes, pledges, and vows (Leviticus 23:37-38).

It's tragic that many Christians are being robbed of God's intended blessings because they think the Old Covenant promises don't apply to them anymore. God still promises that if we obey Him, He will protect us, guide us, provide for us, heal us, and keep us!

So take a step of faith and obedience...come before God to honor Him with your worship...prepare Him a special offering...*then* trust that your amazing season of miracles and blessings is at hand!

Give Him What Belongs to Him!

The Bible repeatedly declares that God is the ultimate source of *everything* we have:

> *Every good thing given and every perfect gift is from above, coming down from the Father of lights* (James 1:17).

> *You shall remember the LORD your God, for it is He who is giving you power to make wealth, that He may confirm His covenant which He swore to your fathers, as it is this day* (Deuteronomy 8:18).

Verses like these are a great reminder that none of us is truly a "self-made" person, nor can we claim credit for any financial success we've achieved. Our material blessings have come "*from above,*" from our Heavenly Father. He has given us "*power to make wealth,*" for which we should be extremely grateful.

Because our blessings all have come from the Lord, He should get the glory for every good thing that appears in our lives. And in the end, everything goes *back* to Him:

> *From Him* and *through Him* and *to Him* are *all* things.
> *To Him be the* *glory* *forever* (Romans 11:36).

In light of such verses, isn't it silly for God's children to complain when a preacher encourages us to sow tithes and offerings into the Kingdom? I can hear it now: "Edith, I can't believe they're trying to get our money again!"

> *Somehow it has never dawned on some of us that it's not "our" money at all! Let me say it again: Everything comes from God and ultimately belongs to Him.*

> *The earth is the LORD's, and* *all* *it contains, the world, and those who dwell in it* (Psalm 24:1).

> *Yours, O LORD, is the greatness and the power and the glory and the victory and the majesty, indeed* *everything* *that is in the heavens and the earth;* *Yours* *is the dominion, O LORD, and You exalt Yourself as head over all* (1 Chronicles 29:11).

Who Paid for the Skittles?

The story is told of a man who took his young daughter to her first baseball game. Although she wasn't particularly interested in the game, she *loved* Skittles and was thrilled when a vendor approached their aisle.

The father gladly bought her some Skittles and then asked if she would share some with him. However, the little girl refused, saying, "No, Daddy, they're MINE!"

The girl's dad had purchased the Skittles in the first place, but now she claimed exclusive ownership over them. The father wasn't asking for much, but he expected his daughter to honor their relationship and acknowledge that he was the source of everything she had.

How sad that many of us Believers act in the same way toward our Heavenly Father. It pains us to give tithes and offerings, even though we would have *nothing at all* without God's blessing.

My friend, God's intent is never to get something *from* you. He is always trying to get something *to* you.

I encourage you to take a few minutes and do this important little exercise:

- *First, look at your hands and clench them, making two fists.* This is the posture of those of us who hoard our blessings. However, there's a problem with this picture: If our hands are clenched to hold on to what we have, our hands won't be in a position to receive anything more. Even worse, we're likely to *squash* the things we hang on to if we squeeze them too tightly.

- *Now, unclench your fists, and hold your hands with palms facing upward.* You're no longer hanging on to any-thing, which may make you feel insecure or vulnerable at first. But realize this: When you open up your hands and release all you have to God, your hands are now in a position to receive back from Him an abundance of blessings—More Than Enough!

Blessing the World

Just as we must open our hands to the Lord, releasing our lives and possessions into His care, the Bible also instructs to open our hands to bless others. Instead of being miserly and trying to hang on to what we have, we're told: *"A generous man will prosper; he who refreshes others will himself be refreshed"* (Proverbs 11:25 NIV).

And the Scriptures give special promises to those who are generous to the poor:

> *He who is kind to the poor lends to the LORD, and he will reward him for what he has done* (Proverbs 19:17 NIV).

*If there is among you a poor man of your brethren, within any of the gates in your land which the L*ORD *your God is giving you, you shall not harden your heart nor shut your hand from your poor brother, but you shall open your hand wide to him and willingly lend him sufficient for his need, whatever he needs…You shall surely give to him, and your heart should not be grieved when you give to him, because* **for this thing the LORD your God will bless you in all your works and in all to which you put your hand** (Deuteronomy 15:7-8, 10).

These are great promises, aren't they? If we are attentive to the needs of the poor, God says He will bless us in all our works and in everything we put our hands to do.

God blesses us so we can be a blessing to others (Genesis 12:2). And the more we set our hearts to bless God's Kingdom and people in need, the *more* He will bless us in return.

Some Christians, displaying either ignorance or false humility, like to say, "Oh, I never ask God to bless me. That would be selfish." Yet it's even MORE selfish for God's people to remain in poverty and financial lack, because then we'll have nothing to give to others.

Mother Teresa was renowned for her simple lifestyle and ministry to the poor. But few people realize that her generosity was only possible because she raised MILLIONS of dollars each year for her humanitarian outreaches!

The psalmist, likewise, boldly declares his need for God's blessing—not just for his own sake but so that the world may be blessed through his life:

*God be merciful to us and **bless us**,*
And cause His face to shine upon us, Selah
That Your way may be known on earth,
Your salvation among all nations…

*God shall **bless us**,*
　　And all the ends of the earth shall fear Him
(Psalm 67:1-2, 7).

The psalmist knew that salvation could only go out to the ends of the earth if God *first* blessed His people. So don't be afraid to ASK God to bless you! He wants to bless you so abundantly that people all over the world are touched by your example and generosity.

You don't have to twist God's arm to receive His blessings. He's *eager* to bless you—not just financially, but also in your health, relationships, and peace of mind. He knows that the more you prosper, the more people will observe His blessings and recognize what a great Heavenly Father He is.

Like any father, God wants to be proud of His kids. If your son was the championship quarterback in the Super Bowl, you would proudly tell your friends, "That's my boy!" In the same way, God wants us to live such victorious lives that the world will take notice.

So even if you've never thought of Biblical prosperity as something you should pursue, remember that the world is watching. People want to see whether God truly is a Heavenly Father who's faithful to take care of His children. He wants to bless you in extraordinary ways, so you can amaze the world and make an extraordinary impact for His Kingdom.

"Behold, as the eyes of servants look to the hand of their
masters, As the eyes of a maid to the hand of her
mistress, So our eyes look to the LORD our God."

– Psalm 123:1-2

CHAPTER 8

WHAT MUST YOU *DO* TO BE BLESSED?

Living the abundant life begins with a clear revelation of the truth that God loves you and wants to bless you so you can be a blessing to others. Yet why do some Believers who acknowledge this principle still not experience a life of prosperity and overflowing abundance?

Often the problem is that people attempt to claim God's *promises* without fulfilling His *conditions*.

Just as the Philippian jailer asked Paul and Silas, *"What must I do to be SAVED?"* (Acts 16:30), after salvation God's people should ask *another* question: "What must I do to be *BLESSED*?"

You see, God will gladly do *His* part to prosper you, but He also expects you to do *your* part. Just as He's given you instructions for receiving His forgiveness and salvation in Jesus, He's *also* given you specific instructions for receiving His covenant blessings.

As the jailer asked Paul and Silas regarding salvation, we must ask today regarding a life of prosperity: *"What must I DO..."* Why? Because God's promises are *conditional* rather than automatic. He says *He* will do this, if *we* do that.

Sadly, though, many Christians expect to receive God's abundance without meeting His conditions. No wonder we end up frustrated or disillusioned.

God's Blessing Contract

This book is not just about God's desire to bless His people, but it's also about understanding His prescribed *methods* for obtaining those blessings. Just like the law of gravity and other natural laws that govern the universe, there are *spiritual* laws that govern God's blessings. And like gravity, His spiritual laws work whether you believe in them or not.

Throughout Scripture, we're told God's blessings flow to those who are obedient to His commands and statutes. *"If you are willing and obedient,"* the prophet Isaiah says, *"you shall eat the good of the land"* (Isaiah 1:19).

Much of God's Word is written like a contract. If we are faithful to do the things He has asked us to do, we have a right to place a "demand" on God to fulfill His promises. In the courts of law, this is like when a party to a contract demands "specific performance" of its terms. In order to win his case, he must first show evidence that he's fulfilled his *own* obligations under the contract.

If you aren't experiencing God's abundance in your life right now, take some time to meditate on the Scriptural principles I cite in this book. In addition to reviewing His promises to bless you, also take time to consider what He's asking you to DO in order to access those blessings.

The Lord's recipe for prosperity has a number of ingredients, and they are absolutely critical to your success. Have you ever tried to bake something, only to realize you left out a key ingredient? Then it shouldn't surprise you that the *ingredients* you include or omit will determine the *outcome*.

Expectancy

One vital ingredient for unlocking God's covenant blessings is *expectancy*. That's why David writes, *"My soul, wait silently for God alone, for my expectation is from Him"* (Psalm 62:5). Because of our confident expectation that the Lord wants to bless us, we can await the fulfillment of His promises with *"faith and patience"* (Hebrews 6:12).

But keep in mind that this attitude of expectancy must be focused on receiving from the Lord, not from some human source:

> *The eyes of all look expectantly to You,*
> *And You give them their food in due season.*
> *You open Your hand*
> *And satisfy the desire of every living thing*
> (Psalm 145:15-16).

> *Unto You I lift up my eyes,*
> *O You who dwell in the heavens.*
> *Behold, as the eyes of servants look to the hand of their masters,*
> *As the eyes of a maid to the hand of her mistress,*
> *So our eyes look to the LORD our God...* (Psalm 123:1-2).

> *Let us fix our eyes on Jesus, the author and perfecter*
> *of our faith* (Hebrews 12:2 NIV).

In contrast to these clear exhortations to fix our eyes on the Lord, it's easy to focus instead on our circumstances and needs. When we do this, our faith and expectancy will nosedive, and we'll not receive the full measure of God's intended blessings (James 1:6-7).

What's in Your Hand?

If you want God to release the amazing abundance in *His* hands, then you first must release whatever resources you're holding in *your* hands.

Your resources may not look like much, but that's not the point. God will bless what you give Him…but you must give Him what He asks for!

The Scriptures are full of stories about God asking people to give Him something He could transform or multiply. Here are just a few examples:

- **Abraham was asked to put his son Isaac on the altar** (Genesis 22:1-18). As a result of his obedience, the Lord revealed Himself to Abraham as *Yahweh Yireh*, *"The-LORD-Will-Provide"* (v. 14), and promised: *"In your seed all the nations of the earth shall be blessed"* (v. 18).

- **Moses was asked to lay down his shepherd's rod** (Exodus 4:1-5). After this event, the simple piece of wood was transformed into *"the rod of God"* (Exodus 4:20). Moses used it to bring God's judgment on the Egyptians (Exodus 9:23, 10:13), part the Red Sea (Exodus 14:16), bring gushing water out of a rock (Exodus 17:5-6), and defeat enemy armies (Exodus 17:8-13).

- **A boy was asked to give up his five loaves of bread and two fish** (John 6:5-13). How many people could have been fed by these meager resources under normal circumstances? One or two? Maybe three? But when this boy's small supply of food was placed in Jesus' hands and blessed by Him, *thousands* of hungry people were fed! Even more remarkable, the disciples were able to gather up 12 full baskets of *leftovers*. What a testimony to the kind of overflowing abundance God intends for His people!

Although I could point to a lot more stories like this in God's Word, I hope you already get the point: The Lord will do amazing things with the resources you entrust into His hands.

"*Whatever a man sows, that he will also reap.*"
– Galatians 6:7

CHAPTER 9

SHOULD YOU GIVE TO GET?

Sometimes people say when they hear me teach about God's prosperity principles, "But David, I don't believe we should *give* in order to *get*." This is probably one of the biggest areas of misunderstanding concerning the Lord's methods for prospering His people.

Some of the confusion comes from misapplying Jesus' words about not expecting people to give us something in return when we lend to them or show them kindness (Luke 6:34-35). This is a very important teaching, because we often end up disappointed when we put our hopes in *people* to return our generosity or kindness. Too often, people let us down, don't they?

However, in this same passage, Jesus teaches that you can expect something *amazing* to happen when you give freely to other people. Rather than worrying about whether the *people* repay you, He says your *Heavenly Father* will notice, and *"your reward will be great."* So the meaning is exactly the *opposite* of the claims of Christians who don't think we should "give to get."

Many other illustrations can be cited about "giving to get":

- Do we sow seeds of respect to others and expect to be treated respectfully in return? Certainly.

- Do we sow seeds of love into our families and hope to reap a harvest of love in return? Absolutely.

- Do we sow our time and skill into our jobs in expectation of reaping a paycheck at the end of the week? Definitely.

These are just a few examples that could be cited to show that all of us DO, in fact, sow seeds in order to reap particular harvests. Instead of being something out of the ordinary, we do this all the time.

Your Harvest Is Certain

To those who insist on claiming, "I don't give to get," I say, "Be prepared for your harvest anyway, because God's Word is clear: Those who sow, *will* reap."

> *Do not be deceived, God is not mocked; for whatever a man sows, that he WILL also reap. For he who sows to his flesh WILL of the flesh reap corruption, but he who sows to the Spirit WILL of the Spirit reap everlasting life* (Galatians 6:7-8).

The laws of sowing and reaping *work*—whether people believe them or not. That's one of the reasons many atheists and agnostics are prospering financially. They've unwittingly stumbled upon, and employed, some of God's principles for financial abundance!

But of course, your faith also plays a role. If you sow seeds without any expectation of reaping, your unbelief may negate some of God's intended harvest for you.

I'm also convinced many people miss their harvest simply because they're not looking for it. Jesus warned that some people *"did not recognize the time of [their] visitation"* (Luke 19:44 NASB). What a sad commentary!

Blessings Resulting from Tithing

Oral Roberts, one of the late fathers of the faith, used to say, "Tithing is not a debt you owe but a seed you sow!" Like few others, he understood that when Believers give their tithes and offerings to the Lord, they should *expect* God's provision in return.

Yet most Christians seem to give their tithes with no thought of how God will bless them as a result. Many give merely out of obligation, with little faith or expectancy attached to their giving.

"But David," you may protest, "aren't we supposed to give just because we love the Lord, without expecting anything in return?"

Friend, though this question may appear very spiritual and noble, it's not based on Scripture. *God Himself* encourages you to bring Him your tithes and offerings so He can bless you!

Malachi 3:10-12 is literally *packed* with promises from God about the blessings of tithing. And for those who may be skeptical, the Lord says, *"Try Me now in this"* (v. 10). Other translations say:

"Prove Me now" (KJV)

"Test me in this" (NIV)

"Put me to the test" (ESV)

"Test Me now in this" (NASB)

In no other passage of Scripture does God tell us to put Him to the test! If we do so with our tithes and offerings—with a heart of expectancy—He promises that FIVE incredible blessings will come our way:

1. He will open up *"the windows of heaven"* on our behalf (v. 10).

2. He will not just pour out the blessings we need, but He will give us even more than we need, *"such blessing that there will not be room enough to receive it"* (v. 10).

3. He will *"rebuke the devourer"* for us, giving us victory over the enemy (v. 11).

4. He will keep our harvest and our income from being destroyed (v. 11).

5. As He has blessed us, He will fulfill Genesis 12:2 by making us a testimony and blessing to the surrounding world (v. 12).

If we truly grasp these amazing benefits from faith-filled tithing, we would be *foolish* not to bring the Lord our tithes!

When You Need a Miracle

But sometimes we need more than just God's "ordinary" blessings—we need a miracle! At one time or another, we've all found ourselves needing the Lord to intervene in the circumstances of our lives, giving us a breakthrough only He can provide.

Perhaps you find yourself in such a situation today, desperate for an *extraordinary* blessing from God. If so, let me share a principle I hope you'll never forget:

> *When you have a miracle need,*
> *sow a miracle seed!*

Throughout the Bible, the principle of seedtime and harvest is one of the Lord's primary "blessing keys," and it's a key ingredient in God's plan for your prosperity.

Both in nature and in the spiritual realm, every harvest begins with a seed. So if you need a turnaround in your finances or some other area of your life, your miracle can begin TODAY—by planting a seed in God's Kingdom.

What Is a Seed?

In nature, every seed contains DNA—an invisible set of instructions for what it is predesigned to become. An acorn becomes an oak tree. An apple seed produces more apples. A father's seed produces a child.

The same principle is true in the spiritual realm. The seeds we sow into God's Kingdom have a spiritual DNA that will determine the harvest we'll receive.

Think about it this way: You can cut open an apple and count the number of seeds inside, but you can't count the number of apples potentially represented by those seeds. Why? Because each seed has the potential to grow into a tree producing countless apples, season after season.

Do you need a financial breakthrough? Then sow a financial seed. Do you need God's mercy? Then be kind and merciful to others. Do you need the Lord's healing touch? Then pray for others, and ask God to heal you as well (James 5:15-16).

Seeds are powerful things! But too often, God's people focus on their *needs*, when they should be focusing on their *seeds*.

Your seed is...

- A tiny beginning that God can multiply into more
- Something you give away to produce what you've been promised
- Your bridge to your future

"But David," you might ask, "I don't have a lot of money. Are there other kinds of seeds I can sow?"

Of course. As important as your financial seeds can be—regardless of their size—there are also many other kinds of seeds:

Prayers	Thoughts	Hope
Kindness	Talents	Faith
Love	Forgiveness	Humor
Time	Joy	Help
Patience	Gratitude	Generosity

Of course, God doesn't expect you to sow what you don't have. But He *does* ask you to give Him what you are holding in your hand.

There's a powerful principle found in Deuteronomy 15:14: *"From what the LORD your God has blessed you with, you shall give to him."* You see, God has blessed every person differently. Some have great resources. Others have little resources. But we *all* have something.

In Deuteronomy 16:17, God says, *"Every man shall give as he is able, according to the blessing of the LORD your God which He has given you."*

Friend, although you may be facing serious needs in your life today, the Lord has blessed you with *something.* Even the widow had a mite to give (Luke 21:1-4). Her gift was small in the eyes of those around her, but it was great in the eyes of the Lord. Why? Because she gave everything she had. It wasn't out of her abundance that she gave. No, it was out of her need.

Whether you realize it or not, you're a walking *warehouse* of seeds. The sooner you begin investing your seeds into the Kingdom and the lives of others, the sooner you will begin receiving your harvest!

"He who sows sparingly will also reap sparingly, and he who sows bountifully will also reap bountifully."

– 2 Corinthians 9:6

CHAPTER 10

BOUNTIFUL REAPING

As every farmer recognizes, not all harvests are the same size. The same is true of our spiritual harvests.

Jesus points this out in the Parable of the Sower. The sower's seed fell on various kinds of soil: *"the wayside," "stony ground," "among thorns,"* and *"good ground"* (Mark 4:3-9). The type of soil had a considerable impact on the resulting harvest.

Even though the seed sown on good ground *"yielded a crop that sprang up, increased and produced,"* the harvests came in different sizes: *"some thirtyfold, some sixty, and some a hundred."*

The good news is that we can do a lot to maximize the size and frequency of our harvests:

1. **Consistent sowing.** Farmers understand that continuous sowing will produce continuous crops. They also know the reverse is true: Sporadic sowing will yield sporadic harvests. It's no different when we're sowing seeds into God's Kingdom.

2. **Bountiful sowing.** The Apostle Paul points out that the size of our harvest will be determined by the generosity of our sowing: *"He who sows sparingly will also reap sparingly, and he who sows bountifully will also reap bountifully"* (2 Corinthians 9:6).

3. **Proportional sowing.** Our seeds into God's Kingdom should be in proportion to the miracle harvest we need, because the size of our seed will determine the size of our harvest. If a gardener only wants a few flowers in a pot, she only plants a few seeds. But if she wants an abundant garden full of beautiful flowers and delicious vegetables, she will have to plant many seeds. We should determine ahead of time what size of harvest we need from God.

4. **Costly sowing.** God shows special favor to seeds you consider valuable. If your seed is precious to you and costs you something, it will be precious to Him. But if your seed is unimportant to you, then it won't be important to Him either. This is demonstrated in the story of King David purchasing the threshing floor of Araunah in order to sacrifice to the Lord. When Araunah offered to just *give* the piece of property to David, the king responded: *"No, I will not give to the LORD that which costs me nothing"* (2 Samuel 24:22-24).

5. **Sacrificial sowing.** Rather than being impressed by the size of someone's seed, God is impressed by the size of their *sacrifice*. Jesus took special note of a poor widow who gave everything she had:

   > *He looked up and saw the rich putting their gifts into the treasury. And He saw a poor widow putting in two small copper coins. And He said, "Truly I say to you, this poor widow put in more than all of them; for they all out of their surplus put into the offering; but she out of her poverty put in all that she had to live on"* (Luke 21:1-4).

This story illustrates that God never asks us for what we

don't have; He just asks us for what we DO have. He evaluates our faithfulness in handling what we've been given: *"From everyone who has been given much, much will be required"* (Luke 12:48).

6. **Sowing into good ground.** The quality of the soil where we sow is another key factor in determining the size of our harvest. Before sowing our financial seeds, we should do everything we can to ascertain whether churches, ministries, and nonprofit organizations are truly bearing good fruit for God's Kingdom.

A Financial Miracle Testimony

Let me tell you about a financial miracle Barbara and I experienced early in our marriage after we sowed a financial seed. We were in our first year of marriage and heard an appeal from a ministry that needed money.

We sensed the Holy Spirit leading us to give an offering. I looked at Barb, and she asked me, "Are you feeling like we're supposed to give an offering?"

I replied, "Yes, I am," and Barb then said, "Tell me the amount you're thinking of."

It turned out we both were feeling led to give $300—which also happened to be just about every last penny we had in our savings! This was quite a stretch for two newlyweds who only recently had graduated from college.

That's all we had...and we gave it *all*!

A few weeks later, I received a surprising letter in the mail:

> *Dear David,*
>
> *You don't know who I am, and I hardly know who you are.*

> *But when I was in prayer, the Lord dropped your name into my heart and said I was supposed to write and send you this.*
>
> *I'm sure that you will know what it's for, because this is what God told me to do.*

Along with the letter was a beautiful pair of earrings. We took them to a jeweler who paid us $700 for them! It was a great lesson to us on God's faithfulness to multiply the financial seeds we sow into His Kingdom.

Seeds of Expectation

The Bible is filled with stories of people who received an amazing harvest from the Lord after trusting Him with their resources and offerings.

For example, what was the first thing Noah did when he got off the ark? He "sowed a seed" by building an altar and giving a sacrificial offering to the Lord:

> *Then **Noah built an altar** to the LORD, and took of every clean animal and of every clean bird, and offered burnt offerings on the altar. And the LORD smelled a **soothing aroma**. Then the LORD said in His heart, "I will never again curse the ground for man's sake, although the imagination of man's heart is evil from his youth; nor will I again destroy every living thing as I have done.*
>
> *"**While the earth remains, seedtime and harvest…shall not cease**"* (Genesis 8:20-22).

Notice that it was *after* God smelled the aroma of the sacrifice that He promised to never again curse the ground or destroy humankind. And it's significant that in this same story He established seedtime and harvest as a principle that *"shall not cease"* *"while the earth remains."*

In response to his sacrificial offering, God gave Noah incredible, far-reaching promises that impacted not only his own life but every generation after him.

Stemming God's Judgment

Not only can our seeds bring about a harvest of blessings, but they also can help to reverse any curse or judgment that has fallen upon us.

In 1 Chronicles 21, David foolishly proceeds with a census of the people, even after Joab warns him not to do so. God is so angered that He sends an angel to bring about a plague that kills 70,000 people.

How could this horrible plague be stemmed? David is instructed to build an altar to the Lord *"that the plague may be withdrawn from the people"* (v. 22):

> *And David built there an altar to the LORD, and offered burnt offerings and peace offerings, and called on the LORD; and He answered him from heaven by fire on the altar of burnt offering* (v. 26).

Seeing David's seed offering, *"the LORD commanded the angel, and he returned his sword to its sheath"* (v. 27). The plague was stopped!

Perhaps you feel like you're struggling with some kind of plague or curse in your life today. If so, it may be a great time to build an altar to the Lord in your heart, and then sow a sacrificial seed into His Kingdom!

An Endless Supply

Another great story about sowing and reaping is told in 1 Kings 17. A widow in the city of Zarephath was living during a time of great famine. She had just enough flour and oil left to make a bread cake for herself and her son, and she assumed they both would die of starvation after that.

However, God intervened in her circumstances and sent the prophet Elijah to her home with a miraculous plan:

> *Then the word of the LORD came to [Elijah], saying, "Arise, go to Zarephath, which belongs to Sidon, and stay there; behold, I have commanded a widow there to provide for you." So he arose and went to Zarephath, and when he came to the gate of the city, behold, a widow was there gathering sticks; and he called to her and said, "Please get me a little water in a jar, that I may drink."*

> *As she was going to get it, he called to her and said, "Please bring me a piece of bread **in your hand**"* (vs. 8-11 NASB).

Do you see how silly this must have sounded to the widow? She didn't even have enough provision for her and her son, yet the prophet said to bring him what was "in your hand."

> *But she said, "As the LORD your God lives, I have no bread, only a handful of flour in the bowl and a little oil in the jar; and behold, I am gathering a few sticks that I may go in and prepare for me and my son, that we may eat it and die."*

> *Then Elijah said to her, "**Do not fear**; go, do as you have said, but make me a little bread cake from it first and bring it out to me, and afterward you may make one for yourself and for your son. For thus says the LORD God of Israel, "**The bowl of flour shall not be exhausted, nor shall the jar of oil be empty**, until the day that the LORD sends rain on the face of the earth."*

Fear was the natural response this widow would have to her dire circumstances—especially with Elijah now telling her to give up even the little bit of food she had left. Yet the prophet told her not to succumb to fear, for the Lord's plan was to give her far MORE in the future than she presently had in her hand. In fact, her supply of food would never run out again! How would *you* like a promise like that?

> *So she went and **did** according to the word of Elijah, and she and he and her household **ate for many days**. The bowl of flour was not exhausted nor did the jar of oil become empty, according to the word of the LORD which He spoke through Elijah* (vs. 8-16).

The widow surely could have doubted the prophet's word of instruction. She could have said, "Look, Elijah, your request is ridiculous. My circumstances are far too desperate for me to bake a cake for you." But she didn't.

When all hope seemed gone, this poor widow *"**did** according to the word of Elijah, and she and he and her household **ate for many days**"* (v. 15). Her meager handful of flour and few drops of oil were *seeds* she willingly sowed, and her obedience resulted in a life-saving miracle of provision. And not only did this miracle meet the needs of the woman and her son, but *her* miraculous harvest became *Elijah's* provision as well!

Believe! Obey! Expect!

Perhaps you are experiencing a time of "famine" in your life today. If so, I encourage you to learn from this courageous widow of Zarephath. There are three aspects of her story that have particular meaning as we expect a miracle from God based on His principle of sowing and reaping:

1. The widow **believed** the word from the prophet.

2. She **obeyed** his instruction.

3. She **expected** God to honor His word spoken through His servant.

Believe...obey...and expect—these are the three indispensable things you must do to receive the miracle you need from God.

Barbara and I have often proven this simple formula in our own lives. First, we **believed** God for a certain miracle. As we did, we set our hearts to **obey** whatever He told us to do. Finally, we **expected** Him to perform the miracle, thanking Him in advance for His faithfulness (Philippians 4:6).

Remember: The devil will do everything he can to stop, thwart, or hinder God's plan for you. He will relentlessly try to kill, steal, and destroy you physically, emotionally, spiritually, and financially.

But while this is Satan's clear agenda, Jesus has a different plan for you—an abundant life:

> *The thief comes only to steal and kill and destroy; I came that they may have life, and have it abundantly* (John 10:10 NASB).

"*Then Isaac sowed in that land, and reaped in the same year a hundredfold; and the LORD blessed him.*"

– Genesis 26:12

CHAPTER 11

PROSPEROUS IN TIMES OF FAMINE

Sometimes I meet people who have stopped sowing financial seeds into God's Kingdom because they're going through hard times—times of spiritual, emotional, or financial famine. While I'm sympathetic to their plight, I gently point out to them that it's *more important than ever* to sow seeds when they're going through difficult times.

We learn this principle from a fascinating story about Isaac, found in Genesis 26. He is just one of the many Biblical examples of how obedience, faithfulness, and expectant seed sowing will result in an outpouring of God's harvest blessings—even during times of famine and hardship.

> *There was a famine in the land...Then the LORD appeared to him [Isaac] and said: "Do not go down to Egypt; live in the land of which I shall tell you. Dwell in this land, and I will be with you and bless you; for to you and your descendants I give all these lands, and I will perform the oath which I swore to Abraham your father..."*
>
> *Then Isaac sowed in that land, and **reaped in the same year a hundredfold**; and **the LORD blessed him**. The man **began to prosper**, and **continued prospering** until he became **very prosperous*** (Genesis 26:1-14).

During a time of famine, God told Isaac not to go down to Egypt, where he would have had plenty of food and water for his household. Instead, he was to remain in the land God had promised to his father Abraham.

When we read a reference to Egypt in the Bible, it refers not only to a physical, geographical location, but it also has a spiritual parallel to the world's system and way of doing things. In essence, God was commanding Isaac, "Don't look to the world or to natural things to provide for you during this time of famine. Look to Me!"

Imagine what it meant for Isaac to stay where there was a *"famine in the land."* He faced the frightening prospect of terrible thirst… starvation…extreme lack…dire need…and a barren, unfruitful wasteland.

It was in the midst of this desperate situation that God told Isaac to remain in the Promised Land. With a future that looked so bleak, Isaac could have been tempted to doubt God's love and provision.

But Isaac's faith in God's love and faithfulness rose up within him, giving him the courage to obey the Lord and wait expectantly for His blessing—even in the midst of the famine. He knew his source was God, and God alone.

I've always wondered if Isaac's faith was bolstered by what had happened when he was a boy and his father Abraham took him up on Mount Moriah as a sacrifice to the Lord (Genesis 22). Was he recalling the terrible moment when his dad tied him to the altar in obedience to the divine command—only to have a ram provided by the Lord instead at the last moment? And was his faith still impacted by how his father's obedience that day had led to the revelation of God as *Jehovah Jireh*—his faithful Provider?

While we may never really know what was going on in Isaac's mind and heart when he reached this critical crossroads in his life, we know what he DID during this famine:

Isaac sowed seeds!

Keep in mind that in a time of famine, seeds are very precious. They are the only hope for a future harvest, so you surely don't want to waste them. No one in their right mind normally plants seeds when there's no water, because seeds cannot grow without it.

I don't know about you, but many people are tempted to *hoard* their seeds during times of insecurity and lack. But not Isaac! He chose to trust God and sow seeds in the Promised Land even amid a terrible drought all around him.

And what happened when Isaac took a step of faith to sow seeds in the middle of this terrible drought? *God prospered him!*

Look again at what this passage says. In the very first year, Isaac reaped *"a hundredfold."* And notice that God didn't just bless him a *little bit* for his faithful sowing. We're told that he *"began to prosper, and continued prospering until he became very prosperous."* Wow. Wouldn't YOU like to have a life like that?

Making the World Jealous

The result of Isaac's obedience had another beautiful outcome as well: *"So the Philistines envied him"* (v. 14). Isn't that wonderful? Isaac was so blessed by God's favor that the watching world was *jealous* of him!

Paul cites the same principle in Romans 11:11, where he says God was blessing the Gentiles through the Gospel in order to make the Jews jealous enough to accept Jesus as their Messiah. That's what happens when the Lord takes you into the Land of More Than Enough.

This principle reminds me of a scene I love in the movie "Butch Cassidy and the Sundance Kid." The townspeople asked about

Butch and Sundance, "Who *are* those guys?!" You see, these two men stood out from the crowd (though not always in righteous ways!), and the surrounding bystanders couldn't help but take note.

The world should be asking a similar question when they see God's people today: "Who *are* those guys? How do I sign up to receive what they have?"

So even if you've never thought of God's abundance as something you should pursue, remember Butch and Sundance. People are watching your life to see if the Lord is faithful to the promises of His Word.

Your Choice Today

Friend, I recognize that instead of living in the Land of More Than Enough right now, you may still be struggling to leave the Lands of Not Enough or Barely Enough. But with the right choices, today can be the day when your turnaround begins.

And although I don't know what kind of "famine" you may be experiencing in your life today, I *do* know you have a choice. You can look to yourself...the world...your job...your family...your friends...your church...or your government to be the source of your supply, or you can exercise your faith, obey God, sow uncommon seeds...and then wait with expectancy for God step into the circumstances of your life with a breakthrough!

When you determine in your heart to be a faithful sower, *even* in times of famine, God will not allow you to run out of seeds for your harvests. As you release the seeds in YOUR hands, He will *always* release the harvests in HIS hands.

However, God's harvest blessings only come as a result of faith-filled obedience. Regardless of whether you are living in time of famine or relative prosperity, He wants you to...

- Believe Him!
- Obey Him!
- Act in faith!
- Expect your harvest!

And never forget: Your Heavenly Father loves you and wants to meet your needs and bless you with a life of abundance. Like Isaac, you may even find that onlookers are *jealous* of how the Lord has blessed you.

Despite the numerous promises in Scripture, I still meet many people who are afraid to sow their seeds because they think that once a seed has left their hands, it has also left their life. This couldn't be further from the truth.

Reverse the Cycle of Defeat

Most people are overcome with fear when they don't have enough. The natural tendency when you don't have enough is to hold on to what you have. Your fists grip tighter onto what little you have in your hand.

And look at the downward progression that results from hoarding your seeds:

- As a result of withholding, your harvests stop.

- As a result of your harvests stopping, you grip even tighter to what you have.

- The outcome is an ever-increasing cycle of fear, defeat, poverty, and despair.

Proverbs 11:24-25 (NASB) says, with my paraphrase in brackets, *"There is one who scatters [gives], and yet increases [receives] all the more, and there is one who withholds [hoards] what is justly due, and yet it results only in want [poverty]. The generous man will be prosperous, and he who waters [gives] will himself be watered [given to].*

Remember: Your seed is *what* He multiplies. Your faith and obedience are *why* He multiplies it.

Your seeds *never* leave your life! Instead, God receives them and multiplies them back into your life in the form of the harvest you need. In the process, YOU are blessed, you can bless OTHERS, and GOD is glorified!

So go ahead and jump into the river of God's blessing. Choose to begin now to experience a life full of the blessings of seedtime and harvest. Get into the divine rhythm of giving and receiving, and then give and receive *some more*. Walk in a continual, loving, obedient covenant relationship with the Lord, and make these powerful principles a lifestyle. As you do, God will unleash a new level of prosperity and blessings in your life.

*Let us not grow weary while doing good,
for in due season we shall reap
if we do not lose heart."*

– Galatians 6:9

CHAPTER 12

ENDING YOUR FINANCIAL FRUSTRATION

I'm sure some of you who are reading this book are still wary of believing that God can bring you into a place of overflowing abundance. Perhaps you've spent years, or even decades, in the Lands of Not Enough or Barely Enough, and it's really hard to imagine things getting any better.

Let me tell you a story that may help…

In Luke 5, Jesus had been sitting in Simon Peter's fishing boat in order to teach the huge crowds that gathered around Him at the Lake of Gennesaret. When He finished His teaching, He told Peter, *"Launch out into the deep and let down your nets for a catch"* (v. 4).

There's an important message of encouragement for *you* in this word of instruction: The Lord wants to take you DEEPER and He wants you to reap a great HARVEST. But notice that Peter needed to *reposition himself* in order to receive the intended breakthrough. If he had insisted on just staying put, he would have missed out on the amazing blessing that was in store for him.

At first Peter protested, saying, *"Master, we have toiled all night and caught nothing…"* (v. 5). Perhaps you can relate to Peter's frustration. You've tried so hard to make ends meet, but nothing has seemed to work. Maybe you've sent out numerous resumes in pursuit of a new job, but like Peter, you've *"caught nothing."*

Friend, God understands your frustration today. He knows how hard you've tried. But He also knows that your breakthrough won't come through your own strength, but because of His divine favor and intervention.

Despite his frustration over past failures and disappointments, Peter decided to obey Jesus' instruction: *"...nevertheless at Your word I will let down the net."*

Peter's step of faith and obedience turned out to be a pivotal moment, transforming not just the outcome of that day, but his entire life after that: *"When they had done this, they caught a great number of fish, and their net was breaking"* (v. 6).

What a dramatic turnaround! The story had begun with Peter and his fishing partners living in the Land of Not Enough, but now they suddenly found themselves in the Land of More Than Enough! And this remarkable turn of events all happened because they dared to believe Jesus' instruction and *"launch out"* into deeper waters.

These fishermen had no doubt seen a variety of catches over the years, but *nothing* like this. They were *"astonished at the catch of fish which they had taken"* (v. 9).

I believe this is God's message for YOU today: You haven't seen *anything* yet! He wants to bless you so abundantly that it far surpasses any blessing you've experienced in the past. Just as the boats suddenly overflowed with fish, your life is destined to overflow with God's blessings when you heed His instructions.

This story ends with a beautiful statement that is often overlooked: *"They forsook all and followed Him"* (v. 11). Why were Peter and his comrades able to take such a bold step of faith to abandon their fishing boats and careers? *Because they had seen Jesus' ability to provide for them when they obeyed Him!*

From Lack to Abundance

Peter and his friends had seen a stunning demonstration of what it means to go from the Land of Not Enough to the Land of More Than Enough. Their faith was stirred to put their full reliance on Jesus to meet their future needs, and they wholeheartedly followed Him.

Have you ever seen God do a miracle in your life? It may have been a financial breakthrough…a physical healing…the calming of your emotions…or the restoration of a broken relationship. When you saw the power of God at work on your behalf, you determined that you would put your trust in Him for the rest of your life.

But if you're anything like me, you might need a reminder from time to time. Although you've seen God's breakthroughs in the past, you sometimes need a refresher course in what it means to trust Him.

In John 21, Peter and some of the other disciples were given this kind of refresher course in the steps toward overflowing abundance. Once again, they were out fishing. And again, they fished all night but caught nothing.

This time Jesus was on the shore, and He pointedly asked them whether they had any food. *"No,"* they told Him (v. 5). It's as if they had again found themselves in the Land of Not Enough or Barely Enough—failing to experience the favor and blessing of God because they were living life on their own terms and in their own strength.

If that's where *you* find yourself today, don't despair. Listen for the Lord's word of instruction, and set your heart to DO what He tells you to do.

In this case, Jesus' tells the men, *"Cast the net on the right side of the boat, and you will find some"* (v. 6). And again, the result was immediate and immense: *"Now they were not able to draw it in because of the multitude of fish."*

In mere moments, the disciples went from *lack* to *abundance*, and the same can happen today for you. Listen for God's instructions, do what He says, and then get ready for your breakthrough.

Too Good to Be True?

If you've lived most of your life with financial struggles, I can understand why you might be skeptical that a better life is possible. "David, this sounds too good to be true," you may be thinking. "There's got to be a catch somewhere."

Well, actually there *is* a catch in some ways. But the Bible is very straightforward about what it is: *If you want God to release the amazing abundance in **His** hands, then you first must release whatever resources you're holding in **your** hands.*

Your resources may not look like much right now, but that's not important. God will bless whatever you give Him…but you must give Him what He asks for!

Perhaps you're thinking, "David, these are great stories, but are you saying these Biblical principles will ALWAYS work, bringing any Christian into a life of abundance?"

When someone asks me this important question, I usually respond: "Yes, the prosperity principles in God's Word ALWAYS work—but we have to *work* them!" In other words, there's nothing unreliable about the Lord's principles…the only question is whether or not we've *applied* the principles and obeyed His conditions.

If we are faithful and obedient to Him, it's up to God to fulfill the terms of His Word. We don't have to doubt Him on this, for His Word promises: *"God is not a man, that He should lie"* (Numbers 23:19).

The Lord will do *His* part, that's for sure. Our role is simply to meet His conditions and then stand in faith: *"Having done all, to stand"* (Ephesians 6:13).

When our faith is tested, we must not give up or lose hope. We must keep believing, keep declaring God's Word, and keep exercising our faith. We also must wait *patiently*, realizing that some prayers may take many years before they come to pass.

We faced this kind of test when our son Ben strayed from the Lord for several years. Barbara and I would go into his empty room to pray, claim God's promises, and ask Him for a breakthrough.

At first, it seemed like nothing was happening. In fact, Ben's circumstances got even worse. But as we continued to align our prayers with specific promises in Scripture, the Holy Spirit moved on Ben's heart. He's now a powerful man of God who takes the Gospel of Jesus Christ to the nations!

Prosperity Is a Process

Do you want to prosper in a certain area of your life? Then patiently sow your seeds in faith, realizing that prosperity is not an *event* but a *process*. Jesus describes this in Mark 4:28: *"The soil produces crops by itself; **first** the blade, **then** the head, **then** the mature grain in the head."*

If you've planted seeds in God's Kingdom, your harvest WILL come. It may not come in a dramatic windfall—one fell swoop—but it will *certainly* come in God's perfect time. If you've done your part, you can be confident His "prosperity process" will meet your every need (Philippians 4:10-19).

It's so important not to grow weary as you await your harvest. Whether in the natural or the spiritual realm, the same principle holds true: Seedtime always precedes harvest. The sooner you get your seed in the ground, the sooner your harvest is likely to come—but you still must learn to wait patiently.

I know the waiting process can be difficult, but that's why the Lord encourages us with great promises like these in His Word:

> **Let us not lose heart and grow weary and faint** in acting nobly and doing right, for in due time and at the appointed season **we shall reap**, if we do not loosen and relax our courage and faint (Galatians 6:9 AMP).

> Nor has the eye seen any God besides You, **Who acts for the one who waits for Him** (Isaiah 64:4).

> Those who **wait** on the LORD
> Shall renew their strength;
> They shall mount up with wings like eagles,
> They shall run and not be weary,
> They shall walk and not faint (Isaiah 40:31).

> The LORD is good to those who **wait** for Him, to the person who seeks Him (Lamentations 3:25 NASB).

You can be confident your harvest is on the way—and it's worth waiting for!

*"He who tills his land will have plenty of bread,
but he who follows frivolity will have poverty enough!"*
– Proverbs 28:19

CHAPTER 13

Practical Principles of Success

I love teaching on God's principles for financial breakthroughs, but I'm also aware that some people will get the wrong idea. Just as there are powerful spiritual laws governing whether God's supernatural prosperity will be released in our lives, He also has given us many *practical* principles that will either add to our wealth or rob us of His intended blessings.

Many of these practical insights on wealth and poverty are shared in the book of Proverbs by Solomon, the richest man who ever lived. If you find yourself frustrated about your financial situation today, it may be that you've unwittingly transgressed some of these important principles.

Perhaps you've prayed, tithed, and even sown sacrificial financial seeds, yet your situation never seems to improve. Maybe you've unintentionally treated God's Kingdom like a supernatural "bailout" program and His Word like a divine lottery ticket.

But God has put *conditions* on His prosperity promises, and many of the conditions are extremely practical. Try as we may, we cannot expect God to supernaturally "bail us out" when we violate these teachings in His Word.

Solomon's Wealth-Building Keys

Here are six of King Solomon's most significant keys for attaining financial wealth:

1. **We must work hard and not be idle.** Solomon writes, *"He who tills his land will have plenty of bread, but he who follows frivolity will have poverty enough!"* (Proverbs 28:19). Before expecting the Lord to give you more resources, ask yourself whether you're working hard to cultivate and invest what He's already given you.

   We're responsible for serving our employer well and doing all of our work *"heartily, as to the Lord"* (Colossians 3:23-25, Ephesians 6:5-8).

2. **We can't succeed by sleeping on the job.** *"A little sleep, a little slumber, a little folding of the hands to rest; so shall your poverty come like a prowler, and your need like an armed man"* (Proverbs 24:33-34). There's no such thing as a free lunch! If we want to *eat*, we need to *work* (2 Thessalonians 3:8-12).

3. **We must learn to be responsible in handling our resources.** *"There is desirable treasure, and oil in the dwelling of the wise, but a foolish man squanders it"* (Proverbs 21:20). We cannot expect God to keep blessing us if we're wasting our resources and savings. We merely are stewards or trustees of our possessions, and *"it is required in stewards that one be found faithful"* (2 Corinthians 4:2).

4. **We must be honest with our finances.** *"Wealth gained by dishonesty will be diminished, but he who gathers by labor will increase"* (Proverbs 13:11). In addition to warning against dishonest gain, some of the other translations reveal different aspects of this principle:

   Dishonest money dwindles away, but he who gathers

money little by little makes it grow (NIV).

Wealth gained hastily will dwindle, but whoever gathers little by little will increase it (ESV).

Wealth from get–rich–quick schemes quickly disappears; wealth from hard work grows (NLT).

Wealth obtained by fraud dwindles, but the one who gathers by labor increases it (NASB).

Money wrongly gotten will disappear bit by bit; money earned little by little will grow and grow (CEV).

Easy come, easy go, but steady diligence pays off (The Message).

Taking these translations together, the meaning of this verse is clear: God's path to wealth is not through dishonesty, fraud, haste, or get-rich-quick schemes. Instead, the best way to lasting abundance is through diligent work to increase our wealth little by little, so that it grows steadily over time.

5. **We must realize that earthly wealth is only temporary.**
   "Be diligent to know the state of your flocks, and attend to your herds; for riches are not forever, nor does a crown endure to all generations" (Proverbs 27:23-24). Despite God's desire for us to prosper, He also wants us to keep our transitory, material blessings in the proper perspective:

   *Why do you spend money for what is not bread,
   And your wages for what does not satisfy?
   Listen carefully to Me, and eat what is good,
   And let your soul delight itself in abundance*
   (Isaiah 55:2).

   *"Let not the wise man glory in his wisdom,
   Let not the mighty man glory in his might,*

> *Nor let the rich man glory in his riches;*
> *But let him who glories glory in this,*
> *That he understands and knows Me,*
> *That I am the LORD, exercising lovingkindness,*
> *judgment, and righteousness in the earth.*
> *For in these I delight," says the LORD*
> (Proverbs 9:23-24).

> *Do not labor for the food which perishes, but for the*
> *food which endures to everlasting life, which the Son of*
> *Man will give you* (John 6:27).

These and other verses remind us that eternal riches are more important, and more lasting, than earthly possessions and wealth.

6. **We must remember to give God what belongs to Him.**
   "Honor the LORD with your possessions, and with the first
   fruits of all your increase; so your barns will be filled with
   plenty, and your vats will overflow with new wine"
   (Proverbs 3:9-10). We cannot achieve financial freedom
   unless we follow this principle and give the Lord the first
   fruits of everything we receive.

Traits Leading to Poverty

God loves the poor, but He also holds them accountable for any decisions or behaviors that have led to their poverty. While the politically correct view of the poor is that they are helpless victims, simply "less fortunate" than those who are financially well off, Proverbs cites a number of characteristics that will inevitably lead to poverty:

- **Laziness.** Solomon, the wealthiest man who has ever lived, writes:

*He who has a **slack hand** becomes poor, but the hand of the diligent makes rich* (10:4).

- **Idle Chatter.** Just as hard work is a key to prosperity, those who spend all their time talking will reap poverty:

  In all labor there is profit, But idle chatter leads only to poverty (14:23).

- **Failure to Accept Correction.** Proverbs warns:

  *If you ignore criticism, you will end in **poverty and disgrace**; if you accept correction, you will be honored. It is pleasant to see dreams come true, but **fools refuse to turn from evil** to attain them* (13:18-19 NLT).

- **Addictions.** Many intelligent and talented people have wasted their lives away in bondage to alcohol, drugs, pornography, or other destructive habits. Sometimes freedom from poverty starts with freedom from an addiction.

  *Do not carouse with **drunkards** or feast with gluttons,*

  *for they are on their way to **poverty**, and too much sleep clothes them in **rags*** (23:20-21 NLT).

- **Get-rich-quick Schemes.**

  *Greedy people try to **get rich quick** but don't realize they're headed for **poverty*** (28:22).

  Good planning and hard work lead to prosperity

  but hasty shortcuts lead to poverty (21:5 NLT).

  A hard worker has plenty of food, but a person who chases fantasies ends up in poverty.

> *The trustworthy person will get a rich reward,*
> *but a person who wants **quick riches** will get into*
> *trouble* (28:19-20 NLT).

- **Dishonesty.**

  > *Wealth created by a lying tongue*
  > *is a vanishing mist and a deadly trap* (21:6 NLT).

- **Immoral Relationships and Divorce.** The spiritual and financial consequences of adultery and divorce are enormous. This seems to be more common today than ever, despite Solomon's repeated warnings:

  > *To deliver you from the immoral woman,*
  > *From the seductress who flatters with her words,*
  > *Who forsakes the companion of her youth,*
  > *And forgets the covenant of her God.*
  > *For her house leads down to death,*
  > *And her paths to the dead...*
  >
  > *So you may walk in the way of goodness,*
  >
  > *And keep to the paths of righteousness.*
  > *For the upright will dwell in the land,*
  >
  > *And the blameless will remain in it* (2:16-21).
  >
  > *My son, obey your father's commands,*
  > *   and don't neglect your mother's instruction...*
  >
  > *It will keep you from the immoral woman,*
  > *   from the smooth tongue of a promiscuous woman.*
  >
  > *Don't lust for her beauty.*
  > *   Don't let her coy glances seduce you.*
  >
  > *For a prostitute **will bring you to poverty**,*
  > *   but sleeping with another man's wife will **cost you**
  > ***your life**...*

So it is with the man who sleeps with another man's wife.
He who embraces her will not go unpunished.

...the man who commits adultery is an utter fool,
for he destroys himself.

*He will be **wounded and disgraced*** (6:20-33 NLT).

If you've been struggling financially, make sure none of these traits is the reason. God wants to give you a financial turnaround, but sometimes that must be preceded by repentance and a *moral* turnaround.

Money Matters to God

I encourage you to take a moment to give thanks to God for two things. First, thank Him that He's a loving Heavenly Father who wants to bless you and provide for you as His child. And second, give Him thanks that His Word provides instructions for HOW you can gain a new level of prosperity.

Few things bother me more than the ignorance of those who act as if money is of no interest to God. "David," they tell me, "I'm only interested in my Heavenly home, not my earthly wealth."

Spiritual as this may sound at first, it illustrates a very misguided and incomplete view of what the Bible teaches. The Bible devotes an incredible amount of space—roughly 2,300 verses—instructing us on God's view of investing, wealth, and finances.

This vast array of verses—on both the "spiritual" and the practical aspects of wealth—makes it clear that God is *very* interested in how you handle your money. If you want to know His plan for your finances, just read His Word and start applying it. When you do, He has promised to grant you success (Joshua 1:8)—beginning in this life and extending into the life to come!

*"The LORD restored Job's losses...
Indeed the LORD gave Job twice as much
as he had before."*

– Job 42:10

CHAPTER 14

WHEN YOUR FAITH IS TESTED

Those of us who desire to tap into God's abundance will inevitably have our faith tested at times. Not only is *prosperity* on trial today, but I'm sure *your* prosperity has sometimes been "on trial" as well.

And I want you to know I don't teach God's principles of prosperity as someone who has never had my belief in God's provision challenged by the difficult circumstances of life.

As mentioned before, my wife Barbara and I once had to break open our son Ben's piggy bank, just to have enough money to get some dinner at McDonalds. And we know what it's like to have times when you wonder how your monthly mortgage, utility bills, and car loan will be paid.

But through it all, God has shown Himself to be faithful. Though our belief in God's prosperity has been sorely tested, we've chosen to hold fast to His Word nevertheless.

Barbara and I have found that the biggest tests of faith have come when our circumstances seem to collide with the truth of Scripture. At such times, we've had to make a decision: Will we side with our own thoughts, feelings, or perceptions about the situation, or will we choose to agree with God's Word?

It has to be either one or the other! The enemy will provide us with "lying symptoms" and FEAR (**F**alse **E**vidence **A**ppearing **R**eal), and it will be tempting to believe him instead of believing God. But we must remember Paul's instruction to *"walk by faith, not by sight"* (2 Corinthians 5:7).

This is no time for timidity. We must not back down from claiming our inheritance in Christ. The devil wants to unleash spirits of poverty and fear against us, but the Lord has given us all the weapons and armor we need for victory (2 Corinthians 10:3-5, Ephesians 6:10-18).

When Your Prosperity Is Stolen

While many Christians have never even tasted God's prosperity, others of us have had it for a while, only to have it stolen by the enemy. This battle shouldn't be too surprising, since Jesus has told us, *"The thief comes only to **steal** and **kill** and **destroy**; I came that they may have life, and have it abundantly"* (John 10:10).

Perhaps you feel as though you've been ripped off by the enemy in some way. "It's too late, David," you may tell me. "The devil has already stolen from me, and there's nothing I can do about it."

If you're having feelings like these, I have great news for you! Even though the thief may have robbed you, God wants to *restore* whatever has been stolen.

"How can that be?" you may ask. Well, let's look at some remarkable examples of this in God's Word.

In Genesis 14, Abraham's nephew, Lot, is taken captive by enemy armies, along with his family and his possessions. When Abraham hears the news, he immediately gathers more than 300 men to mount a counterattack.

Look at the fantastic result of Abraham's raid against the enemy forces: *"So he brought back **all** the goods, and also brought back his brother Lot and his goods, as well as the women and the people"* (Genesis 14:16).

What a great story! Although the enemy came as a thief, God's counterattack recaptured everything that was stolen.

Ziklag

A similar story is told in 1 Samuel 30:1-9, when David and his men come to Ziklag and find that the Amalekites have invaded it and taken their wives and children captive. This was such a horrible situation that the men *"lifted up their voices and wept, until they had no more power to weep"* (v. 4).

David became *"greatly distressed"*—particularly when his men spoke of stoning him! Yet David was a man after God's heart, and he knew where his strength must come from: *"David strengthened himself in the LORD his God"* (v. 6).

If Satan has stolen something that belongs to you, I encourage you to follow David's example and find new strength in the presence of the Lord. And then you'll be ready for David's next step: *"David inquired of the LORD"* (v. 8). When you're facing spiritual attack, nothing is more important than seeking God's strategy for a counterattack.

Please notice that David wasn't passive when he was attacked by the enemy. Nor was he content to wallow in defeat or allow the enemy to keep what was stolen. After David prayed and got his bearings, he immediately went on the *offensive* and prepared his counterattack.

War in the natural realm is a violent and bloody endeavor, and the same is true of spiritual war. When David discovered the enemy encampment, he wasn't in the mood for compromise or negotiation: *"David attacked them from twilight until the evening of the next day. Not a man of them escaped, except four hundred young men who rode on camels and fled"* (v. 17). This was aggressive warfare, in the same kind of spirit we must have to overcome the powers and principalities of the devil.

But David's warfare wasn't only about revenge against the enemy; it also involved recapturing everything that had been stolen: *"So David recovered **all** that the Amalekites had carried away, and David rescued his two wives. And **nothing of theirs was lacking**, either small or great, sons or daughters, spoil or anything which they had taken from them; David recovered **all**"* (vs. 18-19).

This should be our vision as well: Recovering *all* that the enemy has stolen! Instead of accepting defeat, it's time to go on the offensive!

The Spoils of Battle

As wonderful as it is to recover what the enemy has taken from us, often the Lord wants to give us even *more* than that! The Old Testament law required a thief to pay back even more than was stolen:

> *If a man steals an ox or a sheep, and slaughters it or sells it, he shall restore **five** oxen for an ox and **four** sheep for a sheep* (Exodus 22:1).

> *If a man delivers to his neighbor money or articles to keep, and it is stolen out of the man's house, if the thief is found, he shall pay **double*** (Exodus 22:7).

This principle is demonstrated in the story of Job. Satan had stolen everything Job had: his family, his health, and his possessions. But even in a fierce spiritual battle like Job's, the enemy's attacks weren't the end of the story! God broke through in Job's life and gave him even more than he had lost: *"The LORD restored Job's losses...Indeed the LORD gave Job **twice as much as he had before**"* (Job 42:10).

If Satan has ripped you off in some way, there's no need to get stuck in a "victim" mentality. God wants to bless you, restore what you've lost, and give you even more than you had before!

Restoring the Years

Some people have been victimized by the enemy for so long that their feelings of victimhood have become a "familiar spirit"—deeply ingrained in their hearts and minds. Instead of just losing a spiritual battle or two, they feel as if they have already lost the war.

If you've entertained this defeatist mentality, God has a new beginning for you today! He's able to restore even *years* of losses from the enemy.

In the days of the prophet Joel, the people of Judah faced several years of devastating attacks on their crops by locusts. Because these attacks were both severe and long-lasting, it was easy for people to lose hope:

> *What the chewing locust left, the swarming locust has eaten;*
> *What the swarming locust left, the crawling locust has eaten;*
> *And what the crawling locust left, the consuming locust*
> *has eaten.*
>
> *He has **laid waste** My vine,*
> *And **ruined** My fig tree;*
> *He has **stripped it bare** and **thrown it away**;*
> *Its branches are made white* (Joel 1:4, 1:7).

Perhaps the attacks of the enemy have left you feeling like this today: *laid waste...ruined...stripped bare...*and *thrown away*. But God knows about your situation and wants to restore everything you've lost:

I will restore to you the years that the swarming locust has eaten,

> *The crawling locust,*
> *The consuming locust,*
> *And the chewing locust* (Joel 2:25).

And when the Lord says He wants to restore what you've lost, this means a life of incredible blessing and abundance:

> *The threshing floors shall be **full** of wheat,*
> *And the vats shall **overflow** with new wine and oil...*

> *You shall eat in **plenty** and be **satisfied**,*
> *And praise the name of the LORD your God,*
> *Who has dealt wondrously with you;*
> *And My people shall never be put to shame* (Joel 2:24, 26).

What Does This Mean?

If the devil has stolen something from you, it's easy to assume that it's gone forever. But remember what God says in His Word:

- Abraham recovered *everything* that the enemy stole from Lot.

- David recovered *everything* that the enemy stole from Ziklag.

- God's law says that a thief must pay back even *more* than what he stole.

- Job was blessed with *double* of everything that Satan had stolen from him.

- In the book of Joel, God promised to restore to us even *years* of the enemy's plunder.

Has the devil stolen something from your life? Your finances? Your health? Your marriage? Your children? Your job? Your vision? Your peace of mind?

If so, take a moment and commit that area of your life to the Lord. Ask Him to give you His strategies for overcoming the enemy's attacks. Take Him at His Word that He will reverse your losses and prosper you beyond your wildest dreams!

"The thief does not come except to steal, and to kill, and to destroy. I have come that they may have life, and that they may have it more abundantly."

– John 10:10

CHAPTER 15

CHOOSING A LIFE OF ABUNDANCE

I'll admit, I get pretty irritated when people substitute their own opinions for the truth of Scripture. For example, sometimes people tell me, "David, I think all this teaching about prosperity is hooey. We need to be content with what we have…even if that means being poor."

By their own admission, their views are mere opinion: *"I think…"* and "It seems to *me*…" And their views are *wrong*!

The Apostle Peter warned of this very thing: *"Know this first of all, that no prophecy of Scripture is a matter of one's own interpretation"* (2 Peter 1:20 NASB), and *The Message* paraphrase says our interpretation of Scripture shouldn't be a matter of our *"private opinion."*

We need to be careful not to put our own thoughts, feelings, or opinions in place of the truth of Scripture! We all have belief systems that have been influenced by our parents, our experiences, our church background, and our culture. But the truth of Scripture must be our one and only standard for *evaluating* our beliefs— about prosperity or any other issue.

Let's Be Bereans

The Bereans were a powerful example of how we should approach any new viewpoints we hear. When presented by the teachings of Paul and Silas, they *"searched the Scriptures daily to find out whether these things were so"* (Acts 17:11).

It would have been easy for the Bereans to just *assume* Paul and Silas were correct in their Biblical interpretations. After all, they clearly were well educated and passionate about their views.

However, the Bereans wisely made even these mighty Apostles accountable to God's Word as the measuring rod for truth. And this evaluation was clearly an *ongoing process*, since they examined the Scriptures *"daily"* to see if Paul and Silas were speaking the truth.

Are you willing to be a Berean when it comes to the issue of prosperity? It doesn't matter what David Cerullo thinks about the subject…and frankly, it doesn't matter what *you* think about it either. The critical question is simply this: *What does the **Bible** teach on this important subject?*

Once we've come with a teachable heart to God's Word and determined what it says, this maxim should apply:

- God said it.
- I believe it.
- That settles it!

Applying God's Plumb Line

If you've ever been involved in bricklaying, drywall installation, masonry, or carpentry, you've probably seen a plumb line. This vital tool is a weight, usually with a pointed tip on the bottom, that is suspended from a string and used as a vertical reference line. It helps ensure that construction is "plumb," or perfectly upright.

Left to his own subjective impressions, a homebuilder would

always create walls that were tilted in one direction or another, somewhat like the Leaning Tower of Pisa. But by using a plumb line, he can avoid errors and construct walls that are straight up and down.

The Bible is a Christian's plumb line, showing us what "upright" looks like. Whether we're considering Biblical prosperity or some other topic, the Scriptures cut through our subjective thoughts, feelings, and opinions and show us the truth—God's perfect standards for our lives.

The Lord told the prophet Amos that He was going to put a plumb line in the midst of His people—showing them where they had strayed from His perfectly upright pattern:

> *Behold, the Lord stood on a wall made with a plumb line,*
> *with a plumb line in His hand. And the* LORD *said to me,*
> *"Amos, what do you see?"*
>
> *And I said, "A plumb line."*
> *Then the Lord said: "Behold, I am setting a plumb line*
> *In the midst of My people Israel"* (Amos 7:7-8).

This is still God's message to His people today! To live "upright" lives in an increasingly humanistic and depraved culture, our only hope lies in applying the Lord's plumb line to our hearts, minds, and behavior. And that same plumb line of God's Word must be applied as we consider the competing views on prosperity and abundance.

Half-Truths Are LIES!

In this book, I've discussed many of the popular myths on the subject of God's plan to bless His people with abundance. Perhaps you've been crippled financially because you've accepted many of these myths as valid Scriptural truth.

Remember: Most myths are based on a half-truth, and *every* half-truth is a half-LIE!

The Church today is filled with misconceptions and distortions on the subject of prosperity, and we all must be careful not to adopt plausible-sounding viewpoints that aren't supported by Scripture.

Some of the lies about prosperity are the result of "proof texting" or taking verses out of context. This particularly happens when we search for some kind of Scriptural evidence to support our own pet theories or doctrines. Often this includes scouring the numerous translations of the Bible to find the one that most closely matches the point we're trying to make.

In contrast to this self-serving approach, the Bible says every doctrine or principle should be established by the testimony of *"two or three witnesses"* (Matthew 18:16, Deuteronomy 19:15). Rather than seeking support for our preconceived positions, we should be seeking the TRUTH!

Truth Will Be Tested

Too often, people use their personal experiences as their gauge for reality or truth. So if they've not *experienced* one of God's promises, they assume it must not be true.

This is a tragic mistake. God's Word is true, whether we've yet experienced all of its promises or not. The Lord is faithful, even if we don't always recognize His faithfulness.

Over the years, I've observed that whenever God reveals a new Scriptural truth or aspect of His character to me, that revelation will soon be tested in the circumstances of my life. The devil will do his best to present me with evidence to contradict God's Word, and this brings me to a critical decision point: Will I choose to believe God or not?

Fear has been described as **F**alse **E**vidence **A**ppearing **R**eal—and that's exactly what Satan, *"the father of lies,"* is all about (John 8:44 NASB). Just as he did back in the Garden of Eden, he will question the truthfulness of what the Lord has spoken to us (Genesis 3:1).

Even Jesus had to undergo this kind of test. The Father had given Him a powerful word of affirmation at His baptism: *"This is My beloved Son, in whom I am well pleased"* (Matthew 3:17). But just a short time later, Satan tempted Him in the wilderness, directly challenging this revelation of His true identity. The devil repeatedly taunted the hungry, weakened Jesus with the words: *"IF You are the Son of God..."* (Matthew 4:3, 6).

Friend, when God has spoken, we can't allow Satan to sow seeds of doubt in our hearts and minds. Yet this is his game plan, and he will succeed if we're not on the alert.

Even as you read this book, the enemy is likely to taunt you: *"IF God truly wants you to prosper, why are you having such a hard time paying your bills?" "IF the Lord truly wants to bless you with abundance, why are you still struggling to make ends meet?"*

Yes, God's truth will surely be tested in the crucible of your experiences. But despite the various trials that come your way, remember: God's Word is faithful, and it must be our sole measuring rod for truth.

What Will YOUR Verdict Be?

In a court of law, once the jury is seated and all the evidence is presented, it's time for a decision. Neutrality is not an option. The jury *must* decide between the Prosecution and the Defense.

Prosperity is on trial today, both in the Church and in our culture—and now you've heard the evidence. As Elijah challenged the Israelites on Mount Carmel (1 Kings 18:21 NIV), so I challenge you:

How long will you waver between two opinions?

As a "juror" in the trial of prosperity, you must come to a verdict about...

- **God's nature and character.** Does He truly love you and want to bless you abundantly, so you can be a blessing to others?

- **God's promises.** Does He truly promise to meet all of your needs if you fulfill the conditions in His Word?

- **The Great Commission.** Does God truly want to bless you in such a way that unbelievers see your life and are drawn to Him? Does He want to give you overflowing resources to help send the Gospel to the nations and glorify His name in all the earth?

My prayer for you today is that you will base your verdict squarely on the Word of God—not on your own opinions or the opinions of others. And may that verdict be seen in every part of your life: your beliefs, actions, words, and financial seeds.

Reflecting the psalmist's cry in Psalm 118:25, I pray for you:

Save now, I pray, O LORD;
O LORD, I pray, send now prosperity!

*"Christ has redeemed us from the curse of the law,
having become a curse for us…that the blessing
of Abraham might come…"*

– Galatians 3:13-14

GOD'S PROMISES TO PROSPER YOU

I will bless you…and you shall be a blessing.

— Genesis 12:2

You shall remember the LORD your God, for it is He who is giving you power to make wealth, that He may confirm His covenant which He swore to your fathers, as it is this day.

— Deuteronomy 8:18

This Book of the Law shall not depart from your mouth, but you shall meditate in it day and night, that you may observe to do according to all that is written in it. For then you will make your way prosperous, and then you will have good success.

— Joshua 1:8

The LORD is my shepherd; I shall not want…my cup runs over.

— Psalm 23:1, 5

Those who seek the LORD shall not be in want of ANY good thing.

— Psalm 34:10

Let the LORD be magnified, who has pleasure in the prosperity of His servant.

     – Psalm 35:27

No good thing does He withhold from those who walk uprightly.

     – Psalm 84:11

The generous soul will be made rich, and he who waters will also be watered himself.

     – Proverbs 11:25

If you are willing and obedient, you shall eat the good of the land.

     – Isaiah 1:19

You shall eat in plenty and be satisfied, and praise the name of the LORD your God, who has dealt wondrously with you; and My people shall never be put to shame.

     – Joel 2:26

Bring all the tithes into the storehouse, that there may be food in My house, and try Me now in this, says the LORD of hosts, if I will not open for you the windows of heaven and pour out for you such blessing that there will not be room enough to receive it. And I will rebuke the devourer for your sakes, so that he will not destroy the fruit of your ground, nor shall the vine fail to bear fruit for you in the field, says the LORD of hosts. And all nations will call you blessed.

     – Malachi 3:10-12

Do not worry about your life, what you will eat or what you will drink; nor about your body, what you will put on. Is not life more than food and the body more than clothing? Look at the birds of the air, for they neither sow nor reap nor gather into barns; yet your heavenly Father feeds them. Are you not of more value than they? Which of you by worrying can add one cubit to his stature? So why do you worry about clothing? Consider the lilies of the field, how they grow: they neither toil nor spin; and yet I say to you that even Solomon in all his glory was not arrayed like one of these. Now if God so clothes the grass of the field, which today is, and tomorrow is thrown into the oven, will He not much more clothe you, O you of little faith? Therefore do not worry, saying, "What shall we eat?" or "What shall we drink?" or "What shall we wear?" For after all these things the Gentiles seek. For your heavenly Father knows that you need all these things. But seek first the kingdom of God and His righteousness, and all these things shall be added to you. Therefore do not worry about tomorrow, for tomorrow will worry about its own things. Sufficient for the day is its own trouble.

    – Matthew 6:25-34

Ask, and it will be given to you; seek, and you will find; knock, and it will be opened to you. For everyone who asks receives, and he who seeks finds, and to him who knocks it will be opened. Or what man is there among you who, if his son asks for bread, will give him a stone? Or if he asks for a fish, will he give him a serpent? If you then, being evil, know how to give good gifts to your children, how much more will your Father who is in heaven give good things to those who ask Him!

    – Matthew 7:7-11

Give, and it will be given to you: good measure, pressed down, shaken together, and running over will be put into your bosom. For with the same measure that you use, it will be measured back to you.

— Luke 6:38

The thief does not come except to steal, and to kill, and to destroy. I have come that they may have life, and that they may have it more abundantly.

— John 10:10

You know the grace of our Lord Jesus Christ, that though He was rich, yet for your sakes He became poor, that you through His poverty might become rich.

— 2 Corinthians 8:9

He who sows sparingly will also reap sparingly, and he who sows bountifully will also reap bountifully.

— 2 Corinthians 9:6

My God shall supply all your need according to His riches in glory by Christ Jesus.

— Philippians 4:19

Beloved, I pray that you may prosper in all things and be in health, just as your soul prospers.

— 3 John 1:2

Command those who are rich in this present age not to be haughty, nor to trust in uncertain riches but in the living God, who gives us richly all things to enjoy. Let them do good, that they be rich in good works, ready to give, willing to share, storing up for themselves a good foundation for the time to come, that they may lay hold on eternal life.

   – 1 Timothy 6:17-19

Every good thing given and every perfect gift is from above, coming down from the Father of lights.

   – James 1:17

Humble yourselves under the mighty hand of God, that He may exalt you in due time, casting all your care upon Him, for He cares for you.

   – 1 Peter 5:6-7

About the Author

David Cerullo is the Chairman and CEO of Inspiration Ministries located in Indian Land, South Carolina — a ministry dedicated to impacting people for Christ worldwide through media. The son of international evangelist Morris Cerullo, David took a less traditional approach to ministry, graduating from Oral Roberts University with a degree in business administration and management. David and Barbara have been married for more than 40 years and have two adult children and five grandchildren.

MINISTRY *Resources*

Call Partner Services to Sow a Seed for Souls and receive
one or more of these life-changing ministry resources as a THANK YOU GIFT
for partnering with us to impact people for Christ worldwide!

United States:
+1 803-578-1899

United Kingdom:
0845 683 0580

Canada:
(877) 255-3205

International:
+800 9982 4677

Caribbean:
877-487-7

Activate More of God's Blessings in YOUR Life!

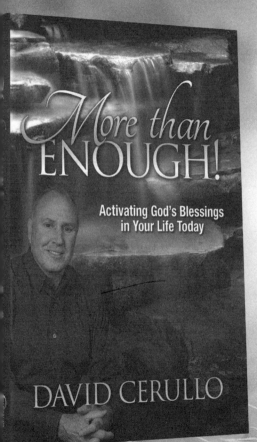

If you're facing a difficult situation today, you're a prime candidate for a breakthrough from God. He stands ready to give you:

- Answers to a desperate situation
- Freedom from poverty and debt
- His healing touch in your body
- Restoration of a broken relationship
- A more intimate relationship with Him

Through the principles in this groundbreaking book, you can experience a life of over-flowing abundance with more than enough of **everything**. That means more than enough energy… more than enough time… more than enough financial resources, and more than enough joy for living.

God's plan is not just to prosper you in some things. He wants you to prosper in ALL things!

God Has Made Appointments To Bless YOU!

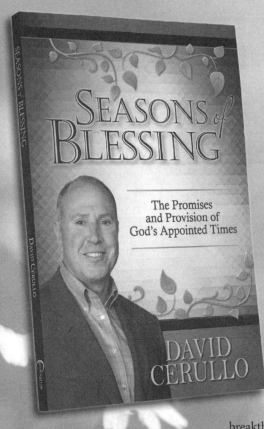

Are you ready to be blessed beyond your wildest dreams?

Whatever turnaround you need in your life — healing, deliverance, protection, a financial breakthrough, or a restored relationship — your special season of miracles can start with a step of faith TODAY!

Your Heavenly Father wants to step into the circumstances of your life with His supernatural breakthroughs. Learn about these special times when He offers to meet with you and bless you in extraordinary ways in David Cerullo's powerful new book filled with Biblical secrets that will transform your life!

"These are the appointed feasts of the LORD that you shall proclaim as holy convocations; they are My appointed feasts."

– Leviticus 23:2-3

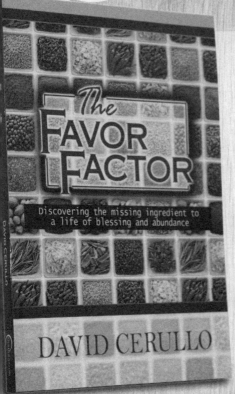

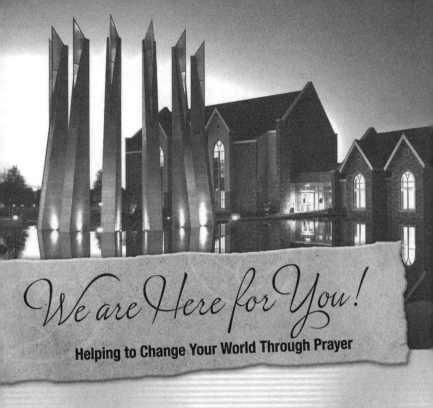

We are Here for You!

Helping to Change Your World Through Prayer

Do you need someone to pray with you about a financial need…a physical healing…an addiction…a broken relationship…or your spiritual growth with the Lord?

Our prayer ministers at the International Prayer Center are here for you. Because of God's goodness and faithfulness, His ears are attentive to the prayers made in this place (2 Chronicles 6:40).

"God does tremendous things as we pray for our Inspiration Partners over the phone. It's such a joy to see people reaching out to touch the Lord through prayer, and in return, to see God embrace them and meet their needs." – TERESA, Prayer Minister

Every day, Souls are being saved, miracles are taking place, and people are being impacted for God's eternal Kingdom! We continually receive amazing testimonies like these from people whose lives have been touched by our faithful prayer ministers:

Debt cancelled… *"After you prayed with me, I received the cancellation of a $23,000 medical bill. The hospital called it an act of charity, but I say it was God!"*
– MELVIN, New York

Son found… *"I had not heard from my son for five years, but I miraculously found him just two weeks after your prayer minister called!"*
– Z.C., Missouri

Cancer gone… *"Thank you for standing with me in prayer and agreeing with me for my healing. The Lord has healed me of breast cancer!"*
– NORMA, Michigan

Family restored… *"Thanks so much for your prayers. I've got my family back! The Lord gave me a great job, my wife was willing to take me back, and I've been clean from drugs and alcohol for almost a year. God is so good to us!"*
– L.B., Colorado

This could be YOUR day for a miracle! Let our anointed ministry staff intercede with God on your behalf, praying the Prayer of Agreement for the breakthrough you need.

We Are Here for *You*

Visit us online today at inspiration.org!

- Daily Devotionals
- Incredible Testimonies
- Prayer Ministry
- Video Streaming

- Video teachings
  from David Cerullo
- Inspirational Tools
- Encouraging Articles

And more!

*This is just one more way we're blessing
and impacting people for Christ worldwide...
starting with you!*